Fin

1

Finding the Oasis Within

Copyright © Victoria Raye 2018.

I am a holistic therapist, a healer and a medium, I work completely from my heart, using not only what I have learned through study, but also, by drawing on my own personal experiences, in order to inspire and empower those seeking positive change.

This book will show you how to free yourself from within and provide the tools that will help you re-take the reins of your life, and to move forward with strength and courage that you never knew you had.

Just as I did.

This book will help you if you are looking to make personal changes internally to create a better experience of this life that you have been given. It will teach you how to get to know who and what you are, to find limiting beliefs and to change what is not serving you well. It is a tool for self-development and growth which can change your life, if, you are prepared to make yourself a priority. It is in no way meant to replace professional counselling or corrective therapy when there is a more serious or medical need.

For Mum
Who's unwavering love, support and belief in me
Throughout life
Has been my anchor

Index.

Introduction

No matter how low we feel or how painful our lives are, there is, without exception, deep inside every human being, the ability to create an Oasis, a place where we are in control, a place where we can find solace, calm, contentment and peace.

It is our environment, experiences, and our own free will and ego which affect our life's journey either positively or negatively. This journey of ours can cause us to create such an Oasis which serves as a sanctuary that we use for renewal and growth or conversely, to bury this inner strength, under such a mound of life's debris that we become completely unaware, even of its existence.

This is the point where we feel unable to make life happen for us and instead, we feel life happening to us. The aim of this book is to help you to re-discover and re-build your Oasis, that sanctuary, within you, the place that holds the strength, courage and inner knowing that allows you to take charge, move forward and improve the life that you are here to experience. We are born to this earth as a Human Being, at no time does this mandatory "job description" state that we are born as a Human "Doing", yet so many of us spend our lives working ourselves into the ground for a future, which may not even be ours, or reminiscing and brooding over past mistakes, meanwhile life and time go on, passing us by.

The past is history- you can't change it, you can only take the lessons and move on.

The future is a mystery – you may never even be given it

Today is the present – so called because it is a gift which has been given to you, it is a choice, you have the free will to experience and enjoy this gift or allow it to become tomorrow's lesson or regrets.

Whoever you are, and whatever your circumstances, just one small deliberate change in your thoughts, can affect your mood, take control of your attitude and inspire you to alter something you do. Just like ripples, which start when a stone is thrown into a pond, these ripples, which originated from a single, happier thought spread outwards, and grow until ultimately it is your day, your week, and potentially your whole life which can alter because, if you want something different, you have to do something different and it takes a lot less than you think, to bring about change.

As an example, a person held in jail, facing hours and hours every day, alone in their cell, can either get angry and disruptive, causing problems for themselves and others, or, they can decide to ask for books, from which they can learn a new skill, or gain an understanding of something that they did not previously know and then, on release, they have built a bridge, which may give them an opportunity to make a completely new start.

I am, myself, a qualified therapist and a medium, however, I am also a person who has experienced some very difficult and unpleasant times. The situation, in which I found myself, and ultimately freed myself from, is no different to that experienced by many thousands of other people and part or all of my story may well resonate with you or somebody that you know. I have chosen, to share my own experience of achieving this freedom and moreover, my adaptations of certain therapeutic practices which I then used personally, to make some quite fundamental changes to myself.

These practices can be used by anyone who needs to find this oasis within them, (this place on the inside, where we can find our strength and ability to make very dramatic changes to us, the person). No matter what your own experience has been, however low or down trodden you feel, by the very fact that you are human, I guarantee that you already have the tools, which I will help you to locate, furthermore, I will introduce to you and demonstrate, methods by which, together we can strengthen, rebuild and re-create not only you, but the very best version of you possible. All you need is an open mind, an open heart and a desire for something better, we will do the rest together.

Who am I?

I am an ordinary girl, born into a very ordinary working-class family. I stumbled, clumsily through life and, not being an academic, struggled through school, never quite fitting in. I started work at sixteen and then suddenly woke up one day, dazed and confused, to find myself middle aged, more than half way through my life, not knowing how the heck I got there, what I was doing and even, why I was doing it.

I had recently hit my "glass wall". I came to one of those "what is it all about"? Moments and realised that I did not value life or myself, neither did I like, or even know the person that I saw looking back at me in the mirror.I believed that I had achieved nothing useful thus far, and that I was simply going through the process that was my life, doing what I felt was expected of me on this proverbial treadmill and, if I am honest, I hadn't done that very well either.At that time, I was trapped in an abusive relationship, I was living to work, and barely getting by. My life wasn't fulfilling, inspiring or fun, so what was it all about? where had I gone wrong? or, was this just all there was?

I know we all go through this at some point or other in our lives, and I personally, had been here before. This time, however, it was my reaction that changed, which meant that my attitude was different. I decided that it was time to alter everything around me, however, after a lot of soul searching, the truth was, that the biggest change required was not external, it was, in fact inside of me. There is no such thing in life as a co-incidence.

My own "glass wall" moment was just a brief encounter with an earth angel. Sometimes, in life, a person that you do not know will just simply cross your path, you exchange a smile, or a few words, and each carry on with your day. Yet, sometime later, you recollect the event, and for what appears to be no reason at all, an unexpected, and often, life changing thought process follows.

Mine, literally happened one day when I was not feeling great at work, and the person in front of me turned around and gave me the most beautiful smile, that, to this day, I have ever seen. That was literally it. I was suddenly aware of how a stranger could change my mood so dramatically in a second, and yet when I walked through my own door at night, it was, without exception, in fear. I knew at that precise moment that I was stuck in a habit, a bad habit, and not a relationship at all, furthermore, I knew that the only way of stopping this destructive, downward spiral, was for me to find strength, something that I was certain, that I had never even possessed, and then, go on to make some major, and very brave changes.

I had never, previously, been able to summon bravery, I certainly could not cope with confrontation and at that point was almost nervous of my own shadow. It made me very aware, ironically that, for once, it was completely true – I was out of control, out of control of me and my life. There would be no quick fixes, no knights in shining armour and no delegation of responsibility. I had to manifest a major change, a change within me, or there would be no change at all.

At the time, I was working both as a Driving Instructor and as a therapist and had been for some years, prior to this I had worked in the Financial Services industry for more than twenty years. I had always done something sensible and had jobs which helped other people, but I suddenly came to realise, that the one person I had never really checked in with, and asked how I could help, was, in fact me.

So, who was I? just an ordinary woman, working hard for up to ten hours a day, six or seven days a week with very little reward. I provided a free home for an abusive partner and I worked when it was convenient for my clients. There's nothing wrong with working in this way, however, I had no boundaries, no personal life and nothing nice on the horizon to look forward to.

A far cry from my younger days which were filled with horses, dogs and socialising, in those days work was a necessary inconvenience which paid for life. Now work had become my life, with no time for anything else, and that included me.

I decided, that if I was ever going to stop my world, with the intention of changing it, then it ought to happen sooner rather than later. I was almost forty-eight years old, the fact that my Dad was just sixty when he died played heavily on me. Whilst I was much fitter than he was at that age, if I was only going to get another twelve years or so, then why was I prepared for them to be difficult, unfulfilling and of no value? As I will explain later, I finally found the strength to change my home situation and then take a step back to look at what was left.

Everything that I have ever done, comes totally from my heart, however, instructing no longer held the passion that it once had. This fact had not sat comfortably with me for some time. I gave myself six months of work, with the intention of then taking some time out to "find myself" a corny phrase but I had literally lost touch with me. It seemed as if the universe was offering me a spring board, so I took a deep breath, a long run up, and I jumped.

As a therapist, one thing that I am very aware of, is that almost every person who comes to me for help with one problem, will, often as not, have other, completely unrelated and unresolved issues which are, without exception, affecting their everyday lives. Nowadays, we are generally, programmed to accept and live with our "lot" In fact, many of us give up on the quest to find a better way because we are so busy, doing what it is that we are already doing, we have no time or energy to find something better.

For once in my life, I decided to make myself important; and my skills work for me, one analogy that I like is that in the event of a plane crash, you can help no one unless you first secure your own oxygen mask. I found a use for my therapeutic knowledge and adapted certain techniques for use on myself to find my own "hidden demons" it transpired that I was personally running a system of irrational beliefs, of which, I was completely unaware. These had been formed by past experiences as far back as childhood. They had been validated over time, by my own experiences, environments, relationships that I had chosen, as well as other life events.

The purpose of our belief system is to protect us and ensure survival, using good experiences to produce wisdom and to learn safe habits which create a frame work by which to live. On the other hand, using any learning which derives from unsafe experiences, to stop us doing that which we don't want or need in our lives. With repeated experience of the same thing, the mind then validates and will continue to strengthen each belief.

Evolution has made us more sophisticated than our pre-historic ancestors and, although life on earth has evolved, our internal programming and belief system remains as basic as it ever was, it cannot differentiate between all good and bad on its own, and therefore, can and does, allow for some negative as well as positive experiences to shape us without our knowledge. As life goes on, we do not know what it is that the body stores, or what effect this internal programming of ours is really having on us. Once found, however, outdated or unreal beliefs can generally be easily changed or removed with a mixture of therapy, positive affirmations and consciously practicing different behaviours. I took a long hard look at myself, inside and out, I realised that I wanted to find out who I was, did I have a purpose? and what exactly I should be doing here.

In my late twenties and early thirties, I had annually visited a Medium, I found this an uplifting experience and without fail, each time that I left her, I felt positive, strong and very much happier. This would last for quite some months. On my last visit, however, whilst the whole reading was as uplifting as ever, her closing comment was a question which scared the life out of me. She said, "are you aware that you are, yourself, born a medium?" With almost a feeling of panic, I explained that I had enough trouble talking to people who were alive and that I most certainly did not wish to talk to dead ones, I would leave that to her.

Stupidly I allowed the fear of that thought, to stop me from returning to her or any other Medium for many years even though the things she said to me, had always turned out to be very accurate. This statement worried me, in hindsight I wonder how different my life would have been if I had only kept an open mind on that day.

I continued my then existing path as a workaholic, just doing what I was doing for a further fifteen years, until the encounter with my earth angel. It was only then, following that experience, and the resultant soul searching, that I finally found the strength to release myself from the second, less than ideal relationship in a row. I had finally reached the point where I knew that I was attracting the wrong people and life experiences. Something needed changing, I looked at every separate area of my life trying to find something toxic to get rid of, eventually, I realised that the source of the problem was not actually external, I had to change ME and from the inside, the alternative was to continue this cycle for the rest of my life which, strangely, did not fill me with enthusiasm.Once I finally managed to free myself from this self-inflicted prison, I decided that I needed some upliftment and a direction so tried but failed to find my previous Medium. I then contacted another whom I had met very briefly a couple of years before. That meeting changed my life.

Her reading proved unbelievably accurate and was full of evidence of passed loved ones and information regarding me that she could not possibly have known. She went on to tell me things which have proved true, and, yet again, also a question "are you aware of the beautiful gift that you have?" She bought up the fact that I was born a medium. This time, I wanted and needed change and a different outlook on life, so I embraced this "co-incidental" second nudge and took steps to check out their comments, and it turns out that they were right. I have since journeyed along the path which is mediumship and worked on my spiritual side and have indeed developed into a very good medium, this has not only allowed me to find another way of uplifting and helping people but has added a further level to my healing work by allowing me to look at my client and my own healing techniques from a very different and unique perspective.

My aim is to share with you, my experiences, and that which I have learned about myself, during the process in which I stripped my life right back to its core, like peeling an onion, using a combination of therapeutic, counselling and holistic methods and where necessary, I adapted these techniques for personal use. I removed layer upon layer of ego, habits and unreal beliefs, all of which, my subconscious mind was using as a blueprint by which I should live my life. My previous beliefs, habits and emotional make up had not served me well thus far, so I then set out to change much of what I found out about me. Finally, I moved forward with a process of creating the person I wanted to be, not the empty shell that I had allowed myself to become.

It was not an easy thing to do, naturally most of us gloss over anything that we find uncomfortable or difficult and, I don't know about you, but my previous dieting attempts alone, proved that I found myself to be the easiest person of all, to deceive. My task now was to look at every single part of me; both inside and out, and then assess it honestly and critically and decide not only, whether that aspect, at which I was looking, was positive or negative, but what effect it was having on my life.

Whilst both difficult and emotional, my journey has taken me from being a "glass half empty" to a "glass half full" person, from a damaged, empty shell to a strong, happy and fulfilled individual. Someone who loves and values her life and the gifts and opportunities that she has been given. Most importantly, I can honestly say that now I fully respect and care for myself. The person who looks back at me in the mirror is someone that I know, I love and that I am proud of, and, as a bonus, I have transitioned from being completely materialistic, to learning to live a simpler, more basic and less expensive, holistic lifestyle. I am a happy, strong person who is grateful for the opportunity of being able to change not only myself, but also my life. Now, I help others who are striving for a similar result.

I hope that by sharing with you here, my ideas and experiences, that you might be able to see how I managed to pull apart the person that I thought I was, and challenge myself, my own belief system, my habits and an outdated way of thinking. I went on to make changes that worked for me. I also want to share with you, the practices which I adapted for use personally and which proved, for me, very successful. They have given me the strength, the ability and the confidence to change my life to one of my own choice.

I have since started to use many of these simplified techniques, very successfully, with clients who need help and direction. If they work for you, saving you pain, anguish and helping you to gain not only the strength, but also the ability, to re-take control of yourself and go on to create both the person and the life that you fully deserve, that's fantastic. If, however, this book does no more than make you stop and consider your own life and its direction, leading you to a happier time in this crazy, busy world of ours, then I have achieved what I set out to do, to use my own experience, to inspire others to create positive change for themselves.

To produce this book, I have drawn on my therapeutic knowledge, my faith, and my mediumship as well as the input into my own process by friends and family. I have used the various experiences that have, throughout life, damaged, repaired, broken and rebuilt my heart, together with a handful of case studies, in order to demonstrate how some of these techniques work. All the personal information detailed here is completely true, where I have provided information regarding client scenarios, all detail is accurate, but I have, of course, omitted any personal or identifying information. I hope that you enjoy this book, and that its contents, in some way, touch your soul helping you find peace, upliftment, and most of all the unconditional love for yourself and others, which stems from the strength of standing strong, independent, and knowing who you really are.

Chapter one
A starting point

It was just after midday on a Sunday in February, I had spent more than 3 years trapped within an abusive relationship, I was four stones over weight and my ex had just slammed his car door and driven off at speed. I was free. I went indoors and cried for I don't know how long, I could never have imagined this day coming. It was almost unreal.

The difference, on this day, was that these tears were of relief and of joy and it was many years since I had felt those emotions. Once the tears stopped flowing I made my mind up that the only correct way to celebrate involved a supper consisting of a Chinese take away and vodka.

On the Monday morning (having taken the day off work, due to anticipated celebratory overindulgence) I sat down, I had a White board, pen and an A4 pad and thought … "ok, so what now"?

I was, 47 years of age. I had enjoyed a good childhood, had a traditional normal family life, and left school at the age of 16 with a very small handful of qualifications. Within just a few weeks of leaving education, I started working for a major Banking Organisation. My young adult years had been filled with dogs and horses and immediately I turned 17, cars appeared. I was independent, and it was great. At 21 I bought my first home, a flat, and between then and my early 30s there were a couple of boyfriends, nothing serious, but I was sociable, independent, busy, confident and happy. I had moved home a couple more times and life was pretty good.

I stayed in financial services for many years, then, following a redundancy caused by economic downturn, I chose to become self-employed and assumed the life of a Driving Instructor. I love people, so the work was perfect for me, and during this time I managed also to qualify in various areas of therapy. Physically, driving instruction takes its's toll on you when you are sitting down, for up to ten hours a day six or seven days a week. At the seven year point it was time for a change.

Now, here I was, middle aged and everything had changed. My Dad had passed away by this point, Mum and I had always been close and throughout my life I enjoyed a great relationship with my brother, so how, exactly, had I ended up, reaching middle age, a workaholic, yet still, up to my neck in debt? I had lost all my confidence, my inner child who was generally "away with the fairies" had been silenced many years before. I'd had no social life since the age of 30.

So, it had to have been that middle 17-year period that had changed me, or, I must have changed myself in that time. That's what I needed to find out. During this period, I had two significant relationships, my first partner moved in with me when I was 35 and out the day before my 40th birthday, whilst he was caring, he was very controlling, and we drifted apart after about eighteen months, and things started to get a bit sour from then on. The second, I met through work. He moved in with me when I was 44, I ignored the early warning signs, he had told me previously, that he could never love me. He was honest, if nothing else, when he also said that he liked slim women and obese women like me repulsed him so, if there were to be any intimacy, he would need to be very drunk.

At this point, I am sure that many of you are saying "so you told him where to go – yes?" but no, the place inside me, that I found myself in, at that point, meant that I had no self-worth at all. I therefore promised to do my very best to lose a lot of weight, furthermore, I honestly believed that, because of the person that I was naturally, with all the affection that I had to give, I could help him to learn to love, both himself and me.

As it happens, he did not want to be helped or healed, he just wanted somewhere to live, somewhere he did not have to pay rent, where he could have his meals bought and prepared for him and where the laundry angels would ensure a full supply of clean, ironed clothes on demand. I was soon to find out also, that he most certainly did not want to learn to love me, he had someone else for that of course, not that he mentioned that to me in the early days, (undoubtedly, an oversight!).

So, as I was soon to realise, it turned out, during this time, I had one controlling and one abusive relationship, both were unfaithful, both also had someone else in their life before me who would always come first. It was not until nearly three years into the second of these "relationships" that I finally woke up and realised something was wrong and I seemed to be attracted to, or attracting, toxic situations.

Some years beforehand, I had been considering a career change. I have always been interested in the mind, so I decided that I would train as a therapist. It was at this point, that I found courses and obtained relevant qualifications and therapy became a second string to my bow. Little did I know at that time, that I desperately needed this knowledge to heal myself as much as for helping others. It did, in fact, become a tool which, following my own experience, I chose to adapt and use for many others but in a unique way.

The turning point for me came when I experienced my "glass wall moment" (The point where you are stumbling at speed, clumsily through life, just doing what you have to do, head down because there is no reason to look ahead, and suddenly you slam into this glass wall, you couldn't see it, and you didn't know it was there, but you piled face first into it, leaving you sprawling on the floor wondering what the heck just happened). Finally, I woke up.

I have always believed that there is no such thing in life as a co-incidence (in fact I have been told more than once that I say it so often, this is exactly what will be inscribed on my grave stone). I firmly believe also, that the right thing, will happen at the right time for the right reason.It was, at this point, I finally realised that I was low, I was weak, and I was lost, basically I was broken. Stuck in a rut so deep that my rut felt like it had four walls, a ceiling and a floor. cast-iron gates without a key prohibited my escape. At that time, I was certain that I deserved what I had done to myself and that this was all that life held for me, so I had carried on doing what I was doing, working ridiculous hours with nothing to show for it and holding my breath as I walked through the door at night, **my door.** Something had to give.

I was sat in my office, alone, one day in September and I broke down, don't get me wrong, crying was a regular occurrence and had, by then, been a habit for three years, however, this time the tears were accompanied by an emotional pain, so strong, that it hurt me deep to my core, I sobbed hard for well over an hour, to the point at which my poor heart, that by now, was so damaged, finally cried out for help, it screamed at me "**Enough!**".

Eventually I went and cleaned the mascara from my chin, my neck and tried to wash it from my top but to no avail. I went and changed. On my return, clean and tidy, finally, I made a decision. That same evening, I took a deep breath and blurted out, in a very inarticulate manner, that I could no longer support or be with my "partner" who was almost as shocked by my words as I was. After a long pause, he informed me that he couldn't possibly leave with the Christmas period looming. Granted our work died over this time every year and, stupidly, I had not prepared an answer for this, so I was forced to agree that he could stay until after the quiet spell, I moved into my own spare room for almost five months, believe me, they were very long months.

It was during the time, whilst I was waiting desperately for freedom to arrive, that I started to adapt some of the therapeutic techniques which I had previously learned, with the aim of using them for my own benefit. I found that I was indeed, holding beliefs that were not serving me well and furthermore they were causing me to act in a way, as to invite bad situations and the wrong kind of people into my life.

Chapter 2
Time to start work

I realised that to extract personal demons, I had to find a way of working which would allow me to be counsellor/therapist and client at the same time. I had to find a way to successfully "work with myself" and so I set about adapting techniques and creating a therapeutic "mash up" which would allow me to find, and understand, how my own internal belief system was controlling me. Your body learns and stores beliefs from just before you are born, and we generally have no idea what these are, until we deliberately go about finding them. If you have an irrational belief, it is only when you can locate and isolate it that you are able to determine both its cause and the effect that it is having on you. Often, this cause will appear to bear no resemblance to the areas of your life which are presently being affected. I will explain here, what I found. The methods which I used to locate them and then to eradicate them are detailed later in the book for your use if they interest you.

The first time I worked on myself using my visualisation technique, (which is detailed fully in chapter fourteen) I got an emotion of sadness and isolation at age two and a blue square. The decision that I had made about myself at that moment was "I am not important "A square has four corners, so I was looking for something involving a unit of 4 at age 2 which made me sad and isolated. For me this was an easy belief to identify and a common one to be holding (however, I had no idea that I was).

There is a 23-month age difference between my brother and I so at 2 my unit of four was Mum, Dad, myself and as a recent addition, my new little brother. Mum would have been nursing my brother at that time. Naturally when the older child has previously had all the attention and love, they have no comprehension as to why the baby is now getting what was previously theirs from Mum and Dad.

Whilst as an adult we can rationalise a situation, and we can see that Baby has the most urgent need, as they cannot do anything for themselves. To a toddler, however, it can seem that we are no longer the sole focus for our parents' attention. The child then "learns" that baby and its needs are more important than they are. For a little person, this can be a big issue. It is the first time potentially that they do not get their own way, and whilst it is good to learn that others often must come first, a negative belief can often be installed by default in this manner. Our subconscious brain is a pattern matching organ, we learn to speak, to walk etc by watching and hearing things repeated constantly, then we try and eventually, with practice, we get it. It becomes a learned behaviour and is then "filed" by the brain. From the eyes of a toddler however, suddenly, their life changes through no action of theirs. The belief that I was no longer important took over from "my parents are at my disposal every time I need them".

Once we have formed such a belief and had it backed up several times, then the brain stores it as simply as it stores the sky is blue, grass is green etc, it makes no distinction. The job of the subconscious brain is to learn habits and to ensure our safety. If, therefore, something happens several times and we have not died it Is deemed "safe", even if it is not something that we enjoyed. This information gets stored as an acceptable belief or habit. We are often driven to repeat behaviours or act in a way as to create similar situations, these then, act to consolidate this belief and very soon it becomes our reality. On the positive side, for example if we are given sugar in our tea several times it becomes a habit, on the negative side, for example, in the case of child abuse, because that child never died it can become a habit the child lives with and is an accepted, albeit, horrible norm. This is how our belief system prepares us to cope within this tricky world of ours.

 So, at the age of two I "learned" that I was not important, because my parents, who taught me all my early lessons, made someone else more important. Whilst it is an irrational thought now, as an adult, throughout my early years, my Brother was always needing that bit more than me, because he was two years younger so to the toddler that I was then, this was a big deal and as a result the belief was consolidated unconsciously.

 I further realised through this process also that I, as an adult, continued to believe that I was not important, and furthermore, I came to believe that I needed a "strong" man in my life and I was naturally attracted to Men who would match this belief. They were very much the macho, alpha male, caveman type, and always had someone more important than me. This, of course, served to back up the belief that I was not important. My brain was, therefore happy that it was serving me well, by matching the "safe" patterns that I had stored years before. All of this happens within the subconscious part of the mind (our mainframe computer) without our knowledge so we are unable to challenge this and change our habits unless, and until we consciously set about finding these beliefs.

 I grew up in a very happy family environment, and my brother and I were best friends throughout our childhood years and beyond, so I was completely unaware, prior to this point, of carrying any such belief. Whilst it is quite a common one to find in clients, it was the last one that I would have expected to hold personally. Once I had found it, however, I could recognise other behaviours which I naturally displayed, without thought, that in various ways, proved to both my subconscious brain, and to the rest of the world, that I accepted that I was not important. I "expected" therefore, other things or people to come first. Equipped with this new knowledge, I could deal with it and I used a mixture of therapy techniques together with positive affirmations to shift this belief, for good. These techniques are explained and demonstrated later in the book.

 The next emotion that surfaced for me was fear. This was quite a strong one and whilst working on it I got a black and purple circle that looked solid and number 23. So, I was looking for something at the age of 23 that had bruised me and that went around in a continuous loop.It took me a while to remember, but after quite some thought, I realised that, at about this age, I had my worst ever riding accident. One week after Christopher Reeve had come off his horse, head first into the ground and been paralysed, I was riding a new horse that we had just bought, and something spooked her. She took off at a gallop in the sand arena that we were in, I remember nothing (medics said I must have passed out before I came off) but I went head first into a wooden 4x4 inch post.

When, during therapy, I asked myself what belief I formed at that moment, it was the last thing I can remember, "I am out of control, I have no power". She had galloped flat out round the arena about twice whilst I was still conscious so that was round and round hence my mind showing me a circle. Whilst that was my worst fall, I have always had a problem with gravity when riding and have been in hospital three or four times and fallen off way more than twenty times. (You will be pleased to know that, although it took me twenty-eight years, I did eventually come to the realisation that I wasn't very good at it and gave up riding horses).This fear experience was validated time and time again with these other less severe falls which formed, and reinforced, my belief that I have no control and I am powerless to change it. Hence being attracted to "strong" Alpha males who were very much in control and kept me powerless.

That one took a while to comprehend, how on earth, a reasonably intelligent woman, could even begin to consider this acceptable. Even though I was very aware that this happens completely subconsciously, and I had treated many clients with similar patterns, I struggled to believe that I had not realised, how I, personally, had been treating myself, furthermore, I was completely shocked at how much precious time I must have wasted throughout my life. Much anger and frustration initially followed this discovery, mainly directed at myself, and many tears were shed upon realisation of what I had allowed myself to endure. Two solid weeks of belief management followed by much positive affirmation work ensued.

So, there I was, subconsciously running beliefs that I was not important and that there will always be someone else, who came first. I was not in control, and I had no power, so along with that came an irrational acceptance that I must, therefore, be weak and worthless. No one, at all, was to blame it is just how the mind. Can, in certain situations, learn things and use these new experiences to change our behaviour. I was, sometime later, to find a further belief which pre-dated, these, yet laid an even stronger foundation for those mentioned here.

It had made me unconsciously seek out certain situations in life and become attracted to "strong" potential partners who would hold the power, ensure that I continued to have no control and would always have someone else, more important than I was. This satisfied the pattern matching desire of my own subconscious brain and further strengthened my beliefs. (job done as far as nature is concerned). I had been living my life for forty-five years, since the earliest belief was formed, acting in this way because I was completely unaware of it, after all, I was a therapist – I was fine, I helped others, didn't I? Clearly, I needed to re-program Me.

Over those five long months I worked hard on what I had found and shifted both beliefs, and I used a huge number of positive affirmations to re-install something of my own character. Once the beginning of February came, I was free, I could finally set about changing the person that I saw in the mirror. A while later, during a conversation with my Mum, she admitted that she was so happy to see me starting to get more confident and back to my normal self, albeit my inner child was re-surfacing, and, as she so kindly put it, I was again "away with the fairies" returning to the daughter that she had known and lost. She mentioned that during the first relationship I had become timid, a bit "squashed" but during the second, I had disappeared completely and just became an empty shell, void of emotion or any meaningful conversation. I had no idea, during all that time, that I had in fact changed so much, but as a spectator, my Mum had literally watched me disappear and become a person that she no longer recognised.

I had been carrying false beliefs, but the truth is, that authentically, I am a very strong, independent woman who is more than capable of running a home, a business and if I wanted (not needed) any one in my life it was in fact an emotional equal and not dictator. Hindsight is the most amazing thing isn't it?

Chapter Three

A Reason, A season or a Lifetime

Many years ago now, a very dear, long standing friend of mine Carol, whom I often refer to as the "wise woman" once said to me that people come into your life for a Reason, a Season or a Lifetime. When she first said this, I thought it sounded very profound, but I never realised, quite how true this saying is. I see the season part of this as a period in life rather than a traditional season such as spring or autumn.

When I look back on my life, it is, possible, to put every person, that I can ever remember being in my life, into one of these three categories. For example, of course, my family are all "lifetimes" Most school friends are "seasons" the first school season, Junior school season and Senior school season, although nowadays, with the joys of social media it has transpired that many of my school friends got in touch after a very long period and we remain in contact with each other in this manner even now, so technology may have "upgraded" them to lifetimes.

The first of my two partners was a season, there were some good times early on and even though things disintegrated after the first year to eighteen months, it became stale and unpleasant at times, but not horrific like the second, and during that time I trained as a driving instructor which led me onto the next season.The second relationship was very definitely a reason. The universe had given me a little lesson in the previous one, and was trying to tell me something, unfortunately I had been both deaf and blind to the lesson and so the universe decided to speak a little louder.

My own favourite line is, of course, that there is no such thing in life as a co-incidence. This is where the "reasons" come in and this is the starting point for any self-healing that is necessary.It is very true to say that life, is not all roses and we all experience times which we would rather not. I have heard the phrase "life's rich tapestry" on multiple occasions; well, sometimes, life "drops a stitch or two" and we wonder why the heck "that" happened. These periods are all life lessons. A life lesson is very definitely a "reason" and we all, without exception, have them.

Chapter 4
Locate the Lesson

From time to time we all ask ourselves "why did that happen? Why Me? What did I do to deserve that? "What the heck was that all about? The list is endless, but you get my gist.

All too often we ask the question, decide life is unfair, cruel or just downright rubbish and leave it at that. We fail to look for a positive reason for that particular experience, or time in our life, and do no more than store any beliefs that we may have formed unconsciously.

Once we have a belief, the mind wants to match that belief. I remember saying to my hypnotherapy teacher one day that the biggest problem that I had was my weight. I said that I had, as far as I can remember, always had a weight problem and that whilst I was constantly starting diets and they would begin to show success early on, they always failed, and things only got worse.

Her response to my statement was to laugh and say, there is your reason for carrying weight. I was confused, so she elaborated by explaining that the brain is a pattern matching organ. When it holds a belief, it needs to have that belief validated by repetition. I always went into a diet thinking 'I wonder how long this will last as they always fail', so my brain picks up "they always fail" and wants to match that belief so success, for my subconscious brain, on a diet, is for the diet to fail as this matches the belief that it holds. I was in fact, strengthening my own belief and proving it correct therefore, I had successfully trained my brain to ensure that weight loss attempts must fail.

This clearly makes sense when you consider how, as babies, we learn our early skills. First, out of nowhere, a big person comes along and keeps standing you up over these feet things which, until now had only been used for sticking in your mouth. When they let go you fall head first into the coffee table, sofa, TV etc but with careful watching of many big people, eventually you realise, that if you shuffle said feet things a bit, you stay up for longer and longer, until you are walking. Speech is the same. So, when we are told time and time again that we are useless, ugly, stupid etc, and we are not authentically strong within ourselves, we form a belief that it must be true. To ensure pattern matching, we are, all too often, then led to display behaviours that match this belief. Ultimately, we act in a way as to prove it which further consolidates what we have "learned" and then this becomes ingrained, as part of our makeup.

When we have experienced these difficult times in life, we often look back years later, and suddenly notice something that we learned, when we do, then we can in many cases "let go" of the pain, the fear or any other emotion that is held in our memory, and the subconscious can re-file it without the emotion attached. By taking a step back and looking at a difficult time whilst you are experiencing it or just after can save years of heart ache, bad memories and nightmares, you can remove the emotion from it consciously and eradicate the sting in its tail.

This involves looking as an outsider at the situation. Acknowledging any learning from the experience and forgiveness. Forgiving yourself first and foremost and then forgiving any other "responsible" person within that situation. By this I mean forgiving the person, not the deed. The deed is done and cannot be "undone" but if you can accept that what the person did or said was wrong, and that they were incapable, at that time of being a better person, you can manage out the negative emotions, hurt or resentment. After all, it is always the victim that carries these, the person responsible very rarely acknowledges, let alone carries guilt, regret, or any other emotion linked to their action, so the only person suffering is you. Why should you carry that for them? they are generally not making their own life worse but by holding emotions that are not yours, you, most certainly are.

As an example. My second bad relationship involved a man who is emotionally and verbally abusive, and, could be physically abusive. The worst and most frightening thing for me, was that he had the most awful, and frightening temper that I have ever come across. He left me in a permanent state of fear. Some time elapsed, even after his departure, and I realised that I was still thinking about his behaviour and that would raise my own anxiety, together with the thoughts about how stupid and weak I had become. I was still suffering and for all I knew he had happily moved on to his next victim. Upon coming to the realisation of how often this was still upsetting me I needed to do something about it.

Eventually, I sat and wrote down what good had come out of that time for me, I am a practical person but this man, for all his bad points, was highly intellectual and extremely talented, he could learn very quickly and anything that he turned his hand to he would master to a high level. He did try and teach me many things. I am not such a quick learner, but I now have a better understanding of my car and basically how it works, I located and fixed a flood in my kitchen because I now have a little understanding of basic plumbing. I am also now able to carry out some quite acceptable DIY and the very best lesson of all, I now know, absolutely, that everything that he felt about me and made me believe, about myself, is completely untrue, I deserve so much better. I also know that I will never again allow myself to be frightened in my own home, and that no one, on this earth, deserves to be spoken to, or treated in the manner I was.

In the grand scheme of things, the three and a half years I spent in tears, in fear in my own home is a small part of my life, but I have bought out of it truth, knowledge and skills that will last me a lifetime. I have been able to forgive myself for being weak and allowing myself to be treated in such a manner, and forgiven him, because his social skills were so few, he was incapable of being a nicer person. I do not forgive how he behaved, however, I have accepted that it was the best he was capable of at the time. I have not forgiven him for treating me badly or making me frightened, but by accepting his social inadequacy, I have let go of anger, hurt and some completely unreal beliefs. I no longer get upset about his actions and it is filed as a very strong life lesson which started my entire healing process. He turned out to be a "Reason" and dare I say it, he taught me the most valuable lessons about myself, that I have ever learned.

Hopefully by now you have realised that although I have been on a long journey, there really is nothing special or different about me. I am a middle-aged woman, I had a good start in life, a quite grotty bit in the middle and found my way out. I managed to get some reflective time and, I changed a lot. I am no longer the person I was, I got rid of beliefs that were causing me to act in ways which did me no favours at all. I found out where I belonged, I discovered my life's purpose. I eradicated my magpie like attraction for the "shiny and exciting" material things in life and have even started to lose some weight. I embraced a simpler way to exist, to live, to shop, to eat and to just be really. I found the authentic me and now I am really very happy with her.

I realised that we spend so much of our time here on the earth carrying regrets, fear, hate etc and yet, the time that we have here, generally, just a few decades, is very short in the grand scheme of things and I for one, now value every minute that I am given, and whilst I generally love people, and will help anyone, and give someone who needs it, every last bit of my time and effort, I will, never again, thanks to what I have learned, "waste" time on situations that do not add value to me or others. My love and time are given in copious quantities but only for positive reasons and not, without thought. I now protect this heart of mine, because I realise how important my life is and I intend to spend all the precious time I have with people who respect, love and value me.

I wanted to use this part of the book to give you an overview of me and my own experiences, by way of an introduction. My main desire, however, is to empower others who, as I did, find themselves in a place that they neither deserve, or enjoy, to invoke changes that make a real difference to their quality of life. I wish to introduce you to some powerful, quick therapeutic "hits" and demonstrate how to use those which helped me change my life.

Whilst this is my aim, there are many people who are in a place that requires long term supported counselling, therapy or medication. This book is in no way intended to replace professional help when it is needed, only to provide support, direction, encouragement and upliftment when self-help is what is required. In all instances where there is a medical issue, then medical help should be sought immediately.

This next section is the part of the book that will, I hope, introduce you, by example, to the techniques that I used and how I used them, and help you to establish who you are, how you feel about yourself and your world. I aim to assist you to make positive fundamental changes to how you currently perceive yourself and others, to help you grow and to discover that you are worth way more than you may be currently feeling. I plan to assist you in making positive and strong changes in your life, transforming not only the person that you see in the mirror but your whole experience of the life that you have come here to experience.It is time to "peel the onion" after which you will have both the ability, and the tools, trust me, to become not only the person that you would love to be but, more importantly, the person that you will love.

Chapter 5.
Let the Healing Begin.

So, you have got this far, which says that you have read the early part of this book, and that you find some areas of my own story, that resonate with you. Maybe you feel that life hasn't been kind to you so far, you might not happy with you as a person, your emotional health, or maybe, you are simply curious. Whatever your reason for getting to this point, then you should be proud of yourself. You have clearly decided that you want change, and, what's more, that you are prepared to do something about it.

There are many people who get to this stage and do nothing, you have shown strength in getting here, so be aware, that you have already made a brave decision and taken the first step towards the changes that you want and need. The next step will be easier as you start your own journey, along this path of yours, to improve your own life experience. The very first step to healing, change or both is to find a starting point and that means looking at you, right now. It is not often that people ever really stop and take the time to look at themselves, inside and out, in order to make sense of who they are. It will, however, allow you to understand what you see, and where, if at all, change needs to be made.

My starting point was to use a large white board, whilst not essential, this is a great tool as everything is in one place and it can be erased and/or changed as you work through this healing stage. A notebook or similar will do. I started with a massive "brain dump" of information, anything and everything that came to my mind got written down in the first instance. This served to release a whole series of thoughts, feelings, emotions, facts and many tears.

These were feelings about me, my body, my personality, my relationships (including family and friends as well as partners), my emotions, my choices, actions and experiences throughout life. Suddenly a whole jumbled mess of memories, facts and emotional episodes, were now looking back at me. This was, itself, therapeutic. Getting these feelings and thoughts out of my head, and onto the board, actually felt as if I had removed a massive weight from each of my shoulders, weight that I had been carrying for years.

Now, however, what the heck was I going to do with literally thousands of words? Looking at the mess on the board, gave me a very real insight into the jumble, that my poor brain was having to deal with, day in and day out. I now understood the mental fatigue, the headaches and sleepless nights, followed by subsequent tired days, which I had long since, come to accept as a way of life. The next stage was to try and get these words in to some semblance of order, so I created rough categories. Your life is different to mine, so your list will look different, however, here are some basics to get you started:

Who am I?
What am I?
What is good /what do I Like about me?
What is bad/ What don't I like about me?
Where am I in life?

Where would I like to be in life
What am I good at?
What am I not good at?
How do I feel right now?
How would I like to feel?
What keeps happening to me that I like?
What keeps happening to me that I don't like?
Why did I allow those things to happen?
Who has had input into my life and why?
what triggered the bad stuff?

There were for me, in all, 27 categories and each had a variety of statements listed. My first job was to go through and find all those which, once I had taken stock of what I was looking at, were clearly untrue. I started by looking for something obvious."I'm worthless"," I'm useless", "I'm pathetic" and "I'm ridiculous" all jumped out at me immediately. Now that I had become capable of rationalising these statements, I realised that it was not a learned behaviour which had caused these. I had just been told these things so very often, that I had started to accept and believe them myself, they became part of Who, at that time, I felt I was.

These were, therefore not beliefs that I had formed personally, from my own actions, but what others had told me to keep me powerless, so I needed a different way of dealing with these labels. I took a deep breath, closed my eyes. I imagined stepping out of my body into my Mum's body. She was the first person that I could think of who loved me totally unconditionally. I walked over to a mirror so that, in effect, I became my Mum, looking at me. I started to list what she sees in me and is proud of. It is somewhat alarming how carried away you can suddenly become, when you "are" someone else. Here are some of the things "she" said to me:

You have worked hard all your life, you have often held down multiple jobs when you needed to, you bought your first property at the age of 21, you own your house, you run, and have created, your own businesses, you are independent, you passed your driving test first time, have a car and are mobile. You have always worked in jobs that help others, you would give the coat on your back to someone who needed it more, both these Men chose to move to your house, you have: provided for them totally, and you look after those you love without question.

Suddenly, although the above derogatory statements were exactly what I felt about myself, I realised that I was **not**, in any way worthless, useless, pathetic or ridiculous. This was a start, so in order to remove these feelings, I stopped there, turned my board to face the wall and walked away. (see the chapter headed "use the eyes of another" to learn this technique). Because these were not beliefs that I had grown up with, I knew they came only from what I had been told repeatedly in the last few years. The way to remove and replace these feelings, required a positive affirmation, let me explain:

The way that we learn anything from birth is by watching, hearing and copying our parents, teachers, siblings, peers etc. The subconscious brain (the bit of us that stores long term information, and acts like a filing cabinet for archives) needs to see or hear something a vast number of times before it stores it as known and a solid fact. A baby traditionally hears Mum saying "Daddy" lots, as it is the word that she wants baby to say first and when the brain has heard it a sufficient number of times the baby copies her sound and eventually Daddy, (or a version of it) comes out.

A positive affirmation is something that we deliberately, sincerely and repeatedly 'teach ourselves' (ideally in front of a mirror but it doesn't have to be), many times a day, for a long period of time. For example, as soon as you wake up, whilst in the shower, putting your make up on, eating your breakfast, in the car at traffic lights, sitting at work on a break, preparing your evening meal, any time really, it must be repeated many, many times a day then again at the end of the day a few times in front of the mirror. It took me about four weeks of continually repeating these affirmations, multiple times a day. After a while, you realise that you start to believe the words that you are saying but you **must** keep repeating this affirmation, word for word until you absolutely know, feel and believe every word that you say. Eventually, I looked in the mirror and said, "How dare they" and I knew absolutely, and completely trusted the fact, that I was not that person and had never been.

Your affirmation can be any positive statement, it does not need to be long, you need to remember it and be able to repeat the same words time and time again. This was mine:

"I am a strong, independent and intelligent woman and my achievements prove it"

The board got turned around, the previous statements that I had just worked on got rubbed off, they were not true and no longer beliefs that I held. I chose two different statements to work on over the next few weeks. Suddenly, I was starting to feel somewhat stronger, a bit happier and I realised that more than one month of my "sentence" had passed whilst I was busy, concentrating on my affirmations.

It was almost November by this point. One area which I hadn't yet dealt with, was my fitness or weight, and, knowing that there was no quick fix, I decided to make a small start by walking in the evening, this served a dual purpose. Firstly, I slowly began to get fitter, my breathing got better, and I actually felt my body changing, and secondly, I was out of the house for a big chunk of the evening. This meant that other than eating, I Spent barely any time in the house with my ex at all, that alone, was fantastic.

I had been very active when I was young and had always felt a mental and emotional high after exercise. This this started happening again, so I was now walking and, more importantly, I was lifting my mood, both with the affirmations and getting outside. I started with some short walks which within two weeks became five miles a night and changing nothing else I lost a stone in weight by the end of January, simply from this new habit, which had only been formed initially, to make the evenings more bearable.

As November turned to December, my board now had a few gaps I considered doing a little more therapy. I could not successfully hypnotise myself I therefore adapted a visualisation technique which works on finding, and then releasing, negative emotion from a belief. I started using this on my return home from walking. The reason for this the timing was that it "does what it says on the tin" It releases your emotions.

Now, some people find their emotional release in anger and can "shout it out", Some can go and do some boxing or targeted physical exercise, however, I cry, If I am very happy, I cry, if I am very sad, I cry, if I am very frustrated or angry guess what…. I cry. Don't get me wrong, for me, tears are a positive way to free yourself from emotion. It sounds a bit like I cry constantly, however that is absolutely not the case, but I learned many years ago that emotions held on to, hurt for much longer and the pain only increases, whereas releasing emotion quickly was the only sure-fire way to get rid of the feelings which surround bad experiences."Better out than in" my Nan used to say, and she always knew best! This work, therefore, needed to be done between my evening walk and my bath, mainly due to the amount of makeup that I wear, and the subsequent landslide effect once I got going!

As I have demonstrated earlier, we all hold a vast number of beliefs which are formed from our own experiences in our early years and throughout life, and it is our subconscious mind that has the job of deciding how to use these. It can deem some memories important and constantly useful, these memories are stored in the conscious brain if immediate recall is necessary for day to day living. If, however, we have grasped something like speech or motor responses like walking, holding something, driving etc this gets stored in the subconscious part of our brain and filed for later use on demand.

Occasionally, however, we have experiences which are deemed by this part of the brain, to be unsuitable for constant recall and then we can suppress memories This is when we know that the memory or feelings are there, but we chose to push them into a mental "cubby hole" in order that we do not have to deal with them now. Greif, painful or difficult situations can be stored in this way.

Unfortunately, if we have something supressed, it can emerge and surprise us at times when we wish it did not, and it can catch us out. Many of these can be removed with the techniques in this book, however if they are very painful, then these are the experiences to be dealt with in therapy or counselling, which will provide an individual with a safe and supported environment, within which the troublesome event can be released and put on the table to be dealt with.

The brain, however, has a further little trick, and that is, when it deems something, way too dangerous for us to face in everyday scenarios, it can completely hide something from us, often something from our earliest years but not necessarily. This is repression. We don't know it's there, we often cannot even recall, the incident it is protecting us from, if we do, then it might be, for example, that we know we were in a car crash where someone else died, but we remember nothing about it. Here the brain has decided for itself and for your safety, that to remember this event would prove, far too dangerous and/or upsetting and as a result, we have no recollection of events or even sometimes, of the incident itself. Repressed events or experiences when unearthed, can cause the greatest damage unless properly dealt with. Sometimes it is possible to find and release them in the manner detailed here but often these events may need long term therapy and/or counselling for the person to work through and come to terms with.

When I started work on myself, I found the two irrational beliefs mentioned previously, "I am not important" and I have no control. I had no idea that I was carrying either belief and no memory at all of my two year old experience which ad clearly been filed very deep but I was aware of having the bad riding accident at 23, strangely, however, I had little memory of it, I remembered it had happened, and the six months off work whilst my vision returned to normal, but I could not get into the memory, it was as if I was remembering something which had happened to someone else, and I had witnessed but forgotten the detail. This one had been repressed as it was a life-threatening experience. I was able to completely deal with both personally, because I had stored them unconsciously and, in each case, I found the belief quickly, furthermore, it was clear that they were completely irrational and were not serving me at all well. therefore, the visualisation method was very effective, and I did not need any further work to completely eradicate these from my own belief system.

I subsequently found two other beliefs, again, neither of which I was consciously aware of running. The first was that I was "not good enough" (having been compared, for years, to an ex-wife who kept the most stunning and surgically clean home, always had dinner on the table and the right clothes were always the ones ironed and ready). He failed to mention at the time, that she did not actually work the 50 hours a week I did as she was a full-time housewife which suited them both. I, however did not measure up to what he was used to. He used it to bully me and I then, as a result, used it to bully myself, I had carried that one since I was thirty-five, the belief was untrue, and it certainly was not mine to carry, that one was easy to deal with.

I also found that "I was disgusting" came from the one who needed a huge amount of alcohol to sleep with anyone, who's bones were not visibly apparent through their skin. This one took a while longer because although I was gaining confidence in so many ways, and I knew that I was not disgusting, I did still have issues based around my weight and my own body image. I did not like the way I looked which meant that getting rid of that belief took longer as I had to make progress on two things simultaneously.

These were perfect subjects for my newly adapted technique.
During traditional therapy you would have been made very relaxed by the therapist and then asked a series of quick fire questions which you must not think about consciously, but just give the first word that comes to mind.

Clearly, I would probably have been sectioned had anyone heard me questioning myself and providing the answers, but more importantly, you cannot relax sufficiently, or properly get into the necessary part of your mind, if you are thinking about questions. You will find the details of how to use this technique for yourself in the method section later in the book.

The reason that the white board worked so well, was that as I released beliefs and emotional blocks internally, I could quickly and easily remove or alter them on the board. Trust me when your board has fifty per cent of its original negativity missing, because you have changed or eradicated unreal feelings or beliefs, it is uplifting and very powerful.

There came a point in the new year and (not that I was counting or anything!) but there were only 17 days left to go until I was free. I had finally cleared my board and stripped away a series of unreal beliefs. I had introduced a good deal of positivity with my affirmations and was starting to understand the real me, the one which had been hiding under all the layers of protection and ego. I decided that it was time that I gave myself a rest, and so for those seventeen days I just enjoyed the countdown to the day that I could finally shut my front door and feel safe.

Chapter 6
Finding Me

So, the onion was peeled and what was I left with? Me, the core of me really. I had stripped away beliefs that were clearly untrue, I had used positive affirmations to set new beliefs in their place, and I was free. It would have been very easy to have stopped there, however there was a lot of work still to do. I needed to change my habits, patterns, priorities and decide who and what I really am and if there was, in fact, something specific that I should be doing. I had reached a point where I had some value and I did not want to lose that, and if I am honest, I was quite enjoying it.

It would have been very easy to continue my habit of overwork, no rest, and mindlessly doing what I was used to doing. However, I had reached a point where I could now, look in the mirror and say that I was very happy with who I was under all that padding, both literally and metaphorically. I knew that, albeit a stone lighter, I was still overweight, however, my therapy work had shown me that I had carried the weight since the worst of my riding accidents and my body was trying to protect me because I was just not listening to it. By understanding why, you are driven to a self-destructive habit, like over eating in my case, you already have the tools to start to change it.

Our bodies, via that little voice inside, that we call intuition, tell us what it is that we need, however, we are often too busy, too lazy or just ignore what we are being told, our bodies, have this uncanny knack of then showing us what it wants, when we are not listening to it. In extreme cases of body "deafness" it will put its own fixes in place, so my poor body had for years, been wrapping me in fat to stop me getting physically hurt due to my relationship with gravity whilst on horseback, and as a shield against cruel words and bullying. All this time, the only awareness of what was happening and what I was doing in response to my body asking for help, was to personally re-classify chocolate as a major food group.

As a therapist you start to understand that victims of unpleasant situations will, very often, create for themselves a coping mechanism. My weight was a result of my own coping mechanism, comfort eating. As I was not happy inside, my body sought happiness, or in my case, comfort from an external source, this coping mechanism of mine served several purposes on behalf of my subconscious mind.

Firstly, as a metaphorical layer of protection from hurt, both physical and psychological. My mind saw me not changing bad things so felt it had to act to both demonstrate what it wanted and to "protect" me itself. The comfort eating became a habit, now, my weight increased gradually, almost unnoticed. As a result, I was proving to myself and the world that I was powerless and out of control of my weight as well, this matched a belief that I was already running.

I had already "learned" that I was not important, so this situation further served to make me feel ugly, and I did not want people noticing me. Putting weight on made sure of that. The beliefs that I was disgusting and pathetic then got formed by what my second "partner" repeatedly told me, again, proving I was powerless and had no control. This is how the cycle starts and then gathers momentum, if not stopped. This is one of the many paths into mental health problems such as depression, low self-esteem, as well as physical illness.In much worse cases, for example, where there has been horrific bullying or abuse, I have worked with people who have no control over what they are going through and feel a psychological need to control something else. Self-harm, addictions to alcohol, cigarettes or drugs are very common and in extreme cases, I talk to people who want or feel they must take their own lives to end the pain of their ordeal.

I am exceptionally fortunate, whilst I went through a very tricky time in my life, it was nothing in comparison to what many others experience. I also had the knowledge and training to wake up and realise (eventually), what I was in fact doing to myself and knew that I had to change it and quickly. I needed to do something very drastic.

I decided that now I felt comfortable and safe, that I would plan to take some time for me. I had always done the "sensible" thing, done what was expected of me and whilst I was not adverse to doing that, I was very well aware that all I did was work to the point of exhaustion and in such a manner that I was barely scraping by so I planned that some months later I would stop work for a while in order to rest and then figure out what I could do, what I should do and , what I wanted to do.

The first step was to get some guidance and so I Looked for the medium that I had previously visited, but I was unable to find her and eventually, I went to someone new, who, again, told me in no uncertain terms, that I was a medium. She bought through a lot of evidence of my Nan and my Dad which she could not have either known or picked up from me personally, and she told me a lot of what to expect for myself too. She gave me messages regarding my work, regarding my own situation, both personally and professionally. She described a dog that had not been born yet but that would come into my life briefly along with many other changes that would come to be, and at the time of writing this book, almost everything that she mentioned has come true.

I left that meeting feeling excited, with a positive attitude and a strong belief, that I now had an opportunity to choose where to direct my life. I felt that I had the potential to make a substantial difference to the quality of not only, the rest of my life, but I could use my experiences, both in life personally and in my therapy work to help others as well.

I gave myself a deadline that fitted nicely with some changes in my own working environment, let a couple of rooms at home and worked my little socks off concentrating on working as much as I was physically able in the knowledge that there would be a worthwhile break at the end.

When the day came for me to stop work it felt very strange, but I embraced it and apart from a little remaining therapy work I had time for me. It is strange how you can carry on for months, even years, feeling ok then stop work and realise exactly how tired you really are. All the years of overwork slowly made their way out of my system. I was not only emotionally healing but I was now also physically healing, and it felt amazing.

Admittedly the first few weeks were novelty, I could get up when I wanted, I could do what I wanted and for just a couple of those early days I did not do very much at all. I had already joined a church and started taking the first few tentative steps towards my own spiritual journey. It was a very exciting time and I had a lot of fun, but eventually I decided that I needed to do something with the information that I had gained and set about finding out what I now knew about myself. What I found was quite a revelation.

Whilst not working, I had gotten into the habit of not having deadlines and my day having no structure. I felt great as I had no pressure, but I also had no goal. I was having a lovely time, but I was "swimming around" with no destination or end product. This in itself made my days very inefficient.As I have mentioned previously, I have a propensity to mentally spend all my time either in the past, re living and beating myself up about mistakes and bad choices or, in the future, planning what I want to do and how I want to do it but without following this up with useful action. This is not sensible, however having removed much of my own emotional "baggage" I started to find some time to read some philosophy and the first book that I read had several very strong messages contained within it and one of the first is a phrase which has stuck with me in a very definite way and whilst I quoted it at the beginning of this book, I feel inclined to repeat its message here as it is very relevant to the time on my journey that we are currently looking at.

The past is history
The future is a mystery
Today is the present, so called because it is a gift and you have been given it.

Becoming aware of the sheer number of hours that I spent mentally "in the past" brooding over what was, what could have been, what should have been, and "in the future" considering what could be and what might be was quite a shock.

Chapter 7
Living in the now.

The very first thing that I did next was to look at what I was now doing with all this time that I had and what I was achieving. The "old" me would get up between five and six am, have breakfast, work for between nine and twelve hours, get home cook, wash, iron, bath and go to bed, then start the same routine again in the morning six, and often seven days a week. Now, however, I was getting up at seven, feeding the cat, then myself, doing housework but I then found myself spending hours a day, deep in thought about two periods in time over which I had no control at all.

I often watch my cat with envy. She sleeps and when she wakes up she will look around to see if I am anywhere for a cuddle, if not she will go and eat food, play with toys, roll around on the floor or look out of the window watching "cat stuff" – she sees who goes by, she looks at the grass and the hedges and no doubt thinks " it's about time Mum cut those" but she doesn't think about yesterday, she doesn't worry about tomorrow, she has nothing to fear she lives totally in the moment. "What is happening now? Ok I will do this then". Animals rarely get depression, anxiety, exhaustion or stress, they live, they play, they love, they eat, they sleep. They don't, to my knowledge, spend hours in regret or planning for their old age.

When was the last time you walked to your front door and stopped and looked at your house, noticed how high you needed to pick up your foot to avoid falling in the door? Noticed exactly what you needed to do and how it felt just to sit down on the sofa at the end of the day? Just looked around at the pictures on your wall and really noticed them, looked at the colours, remembered why you bought them. When was the last time you lived in the now?

This was a question I started asking myself and slowly, the hours of regret and daydreams about what I wish would happen in the future gave way to activity, walking, noticing things around me, living close to the sea, my favourite activity is walking down to the beach at night and seeing the moon and the stars and their reflection in the ocean. Quality time, peace, relaxation and exercise. Doing some jobs around the house that had gone undone for years making the house brighter and more comfortable and most of all clearing out.

I have always been a hoarder – you never know when you will need that again has been heard many hundreds of times in my home, so I decided to have a clear out. Six shelves of books, most never read past page 10 went, over 300 CDs that I never listen to, some still in their wrappers, over 100 DVDs, three occasional tables that matched nothing else in the room went, ornaments or dust traps as they had become, unless they had sentimental value, went, and that was just the lounge, all of a sudden the floor space in that room looked vast, the sense of satisfaction for clearing "junk" out was phenomenal. I started on my bedroom and clothes, linen, toiletries from the last few Christmases that I wouldn't use, more books and ornaments. Makeup that I hadn't used in years and so it went on. The garage and the loft did not escape either, both had been full of stuff which had remained untouched for years, both exes were into taking vehicles apart and leaving unwanted car parts in my garage (more than two hundred in total)– I had to pay someone to take away all this "junk" which was in essence, my past which has been relegated to just a memory now!

So, my daydream time had provided me with a bigger, clearer, cleaner brighter house just by living so much more, in the now. This proved very therapeutic, the charity shops got saleable items and I feel happier in my home now it feels very different, all this activity was followed by redecorating and having some work done which meant that now my house is my home, my stamp on everything and having experienced control and abuse, I can find no words worthy of the feeling that you have once you have achieved that. It takes some practice but there are many opportunities every day to take a bit of time and live in the now, I meditate daily, I used to struggle as my mind was so busy but now I can sit and meditate in silence and the positive effects on your mind and body are dramatic even if you can only spend ten minutes a day, dedicated to your own wellbeing. For further detail regarding meditation see chapter 22.

If you don't look after yourself in this way, what can start as a bit of a worry one day, can, if ignored, get fed by our lack of time, work or relationship stress. Simply missing the bus, the car not starting, general day to day things, then suddenly that little worry is causing you not to sleep so well. This makes you tired and irritable, which affects your eating, which subsequently affects your mood and before you know it you are picking up a prescription for anti-depressants.

A few months off work follow, naturally worrying more as you can't afford the bills and so it goes on, all because we do not give ourselves the opportunity to rest our mind and body and live in the now. If we don't take the time to choose sensibly what we do with the gift of today, we have lost it forever. This is the difference between living and existing, whatever your situation, there will be things that you can do, without cost and that take very little time, but which improve the quality of your day immeasurably, this in turn will positively improve your health.

Many of us eat because we must, but do not do it mindfully, we shovel a meal down our throat, as quick as we can, in order to get on with the next task or even, as we get on with the next task. Many evening meals used to get eaten, whilst I was cleaning the kitchen, or doing the washing up. We often do not even taste our food or enjoy it. In years gone by meal times were family times, to talk, socialise, download your day enjoy the company of your family, talk about your problems or worries, find remedies for someone else's problems. Often three generations of a family might have sat down to an evening meal, in those days nowhere near the need for therapy or counselling existed as the family dealt with everything together, now, most families, once the children are at senior school age, are just a group of people, doing their own thing, trying to deal with their own issues on their own. In a way "progress" has had the opposite effect as society has almost adopted an "every man for himself" attitude.

I remember clearly, that when I was junior school age, my grandparent's front door was never locked during the day and so neighbours would just pop in for a chat or some advice, completely unannounced and "a trouble shared was a trouble halved". Nowadays a trouble shared so often turns out to be at a cost of £50+ an hour to a counsellor or therapist.

So, when was the last time you made time for you?

Chapter 8
The universal law of attraction.

I am sure that you have heard some, if not all, of the following phrases.

What you sow, so shall you reap (there are many versions of this one).

You only get back what you put in.

Your life is a mirror.

Your life becomes a reflection of you.

You only get as much as you give.

What you see, is you through another's eyes.

Attitude+ Effort + Commitment = Result

This list could go on and on, but you get my point. Although mostly, if you mention these phrases, the reaction that you get will generally involve eyes rolled to heaven, a tut or a sigh, they are, in fact, absolutely true. This universe in which we live will always find and create balance, although it may not always be immediately apparent, like will always, if not interfered with, attract like.

If for example things don't go well first thing in the morning – you oversleep, spill coffee on your top, poke yourself in the eye with the mascara brush, the car won't start and you are late for work….you will leave the house feeling a certain way, this will not be filled with fun, laughter, happy thoughts and love for the world around you, but you are more likely to feel miserable, sad, frustrated and even angry. Have you ever noticed how on these days, the people with whom you come into contact are generally angry, short tempered, fed up and down right miserable?

On the flip side, you open the curtains and sunlight bathes your room, you listen to bird song whilst having breakfast and the morning radio DJ plays your favourite tune, on the way to work you notice the smell of fresh bread from the bakery and you see that the spring flowers are blooming. Upon your arrival at work you receive a letter of thanks from a happy customer who did not need to write in, your partner just happens to see some flowers and brings them home for you, for no reason other than they thought of you when they saw them. On a day like this, everyone seems to have a smile for you, a joke to tell or just seem to be happy to be alive. These are the days when your best friend from school calls out of the blue with good news.

It is no Co-incidence, (because, as you know... there is no such thing in life as a co-incidence!) everything happens for a reason, and much of the time, you are the reason. You put out friendly, happy vibes and like a boomerang they come right back to you, similarly you put out misery, anger or frustration, guess what you are going to get. Don't get me wrong, we all have bad days, weeks months…. but we are all capable of consciously choosing our mood. You can think, right, that's it, it's going to be a bad day and guess what – you are right, and all because you decided it would be. You could say to yourself ok, that's todays bit of bad luck out of the way, the rest of the day is going to be great, put a smile on your face, listen to some great music to lift your mood and guess what, this time you are right too– the rest of the day will be great.

I mentioned previously the prisoner, locked up for many hours day in, day out, can cause trouble making both their life and that of all those around them miserable and end up having parole denied due to their conduct, or, they can reflect on why life has brought them to this point and how they can start to make a change to their life and "luck" going forward, they can ask for training, educational books or a job which will not only help others, but possibly also give them a new skill by the time they leave. If such a choice is made, this will have no derogatory impact on them, however it could result in their sentence time seeming to go quicker, or even being shortened for good behaviour and a brand-new start when they get out.

So, what can we learn from this? We can choose our mood, irrespective of our situation we can change how we feel about it, for good or bad! Yes, sometimes it takes every bit of strength that we can possibly muster, but, however difficult, it is absolutely possible. We create the environment that the universe will match, like for like, in order to achieve balance. This is where the previous chapters can provide the tools you need.

In the same way that once we have mastered language, we do not have to consciously think how to say each word, we do not consciously create our moods, we often allow outside influences to affect us – the spilled coffee, the non- compliant car, lipstick up your nose, etc can cause stress and set your mood to low. Taking the time to stop, take a breath, and consciously, decide to fit in a short meditation before you set off for work, or listen to some favourite music, will completely change your mood. This action then, in turn, attracts people to you whose mood matches yours. This is a day changer for you all. Likewise, if you feel like rubbish, subconsciously you act in such a way as to play out what you believe about yourself, right at that moment, so that is what people see and believe. This then dictates the way in which they will treat you and affects the way that they feel about you as a person, this is apparent in their interaction with you, making you feel worse.

Spending several weeks, religiously using your positive affirmation many times a day, is an investment in you. Used correctly it will change both how you feel and what it is that you believe about yourself. This new personal regard will then match the authentic knowledge from deep within your soul (because no one is born a bad person) and subsequently, the thoughts that occur naturally about yourself and your world change. Following such a shift, behaviours that you display will naturally evoke changes in what those around you see, their opinion of you and their thoughts about you.

These things will take time, they will take practice, they will take commitment, and they will take a shift in your attitude BUT, if you make this investment in you, I guarantee that you will see and feel the changes that you make, you are worth it. The best piece of advice that I have ever been given is this: Treat yourself like someone you love. If you do, then the universe will love you too. Believe me, during the time between telling my ex that he was no longer welcome, and the time of writing this book, I have grown, evolved and changed so very dramatically that even I cannot recall the weak, downtrodden person that I was for so many years. If I look at photographs from that time, I can clearly see that I am unhappy, and I look facially, much older back then, than I do now. This investment in you, because you are worth it, will make a positive impact on your life which directly makes an impact on you. If you put in the effort, with the right attitude and commitment you will see a result. The universal law of attraction cannot work any other way, it is how the energy within the universe flows, you cannot stop it, you cannot change it, but you do choose whether you flow with, or against it.

This is the very reason, you cannot stop time, it is on an eternal path, a morning progresses to an afternoon, to an evening, to a night to the next morning – constant forward momentum – learn to flow with this energy and you have no choice but to progress constantly and once you deliberately form new habits and beliefs this happens naturally, and without effort, it is just the way you become, you cannot help but to progress and grow. I have said it before here, but I will say it again. If you want to get something different then you must do something different. It is a choice, your choice, you put in the effort and You reap the rewards. As you can see, everything that you do attracts like, however it is not only the things that you do, be conscious also, of your thoughts.

As far as the universe is concerned, your thought is an action. So, if you need something to come into your life ask for it, please don't get me wrong, you can beg, ask, or even get down on your knees and plead with the universe for a lottery jackpot, but so are all the other six billion people on the planet. And there aren't enough jackpots to go around, however, you will be surprised at exactly how powerful your thoughts can be, when used correctly.

Let's assume for example, that you are having a real struggle and that there is something that you really do need, you can ask the universe. Some people like to go down to the sea and ask out loud, however your thoughts are as strong as your words and the universe hears every one of them, it is important, however, to remember that you get what you ask for. If, for example, you have an opportunity for a promotion at work, but your thought pattern is that you would love it, but you know that you don't have a chance, or you are not good enough for it or that you never get anything good happening to you, that is exactly the instruction that you are giving to the universe.

If, on the other hand you manage your thoughts in so much as you think "I am more than capable of doing a fantastic job in that role and I deserve the opportunity" then the universe will take that as it's instruction and you will find yourself acting in a way to get seen at the right time by the right people, you will fly through the interview and, if it is right for your own growth, an offer will come.

It is important to remember you can generally attract what you need or want if it is beneficial to you and not of detriment to someone else. This universe wants you to have the very best experience of this life of yours on earth, and will ensure that, where reasonable, you will get what you want and need if there is a good reason for it. We, all six billion of us share this planet and we all have thoughts, wants and needs, so do not waste your requests, make a choice to improve things, believe in it completely then watch what the universe can and will do, it rarely happens overnight, however if you are observant, you will notice a series of small changes in attitude, behaviour and all of a sudden, your dream is starting to become your reality.

It is also true, that what you put into life, you will get out of it so if you are one of life's takers, and do not consider others you will get the basic essentials that you need. If you happen to be someone who does good for others wanting nothing in return, it is just how you are then you will find that your kindness is repaid by a loving universe. We all have lessons in life and hard times, but it is not about what hand you are dealt in this life, as we all have good and bad experiences, but the way you play the hand that you have been dealt which will have a massive bearing on your own experience.

So, returning to the "corny" quotations at the start of this chapter, be it thought, request, deed or intention, that which you sow, attracts that which you reap, and there is no way round it.
Many people prefer to use the term karma, this principle is exactly the same. If you are true, honest, kind, generous of nature, this will come back to you, if you are cruel, unkind intolerant, this too will come back to you in this life or the next.

Chapter 9
Boundaries.

Now that you have, hopefully, made yourself important and learned to respect yourself a little more, it is time to look after the new you, time to set some boundaries.In the early part of the book I mentioned that I had let life take over and found myself with no boundaries. On reflection, of course, this fact alone is likely to be one major reason that I allowed myself to experience two bad relationships and lost control of my working hours.

Looking back now, over the earlier years of employed work, I realise that since my thirties I mostly worked well over the contracted hours for which I was paid. For several years, I had worked in locations which involved two hours plus of travelling each day. Add to the working day unpaid hours, fuel and wear and tear on my car I was working from eight up to ten hours a day and out of the house for twelve plus hours in total. So, as you can see, my habit of living, purely to work was not a new one.

The above scenario is fine if you are in a job which is your passion, and the rewards dramatically outweigh the input, but this was not the case for me, and I had been doing this to myself for years totally unconsciously. In essence, the beliefs that I was not important and that I had no control had encompassed my work life as much as my personal life. I had no love or respect for myself and as far as the universe was aware, I was saying to myself and the world that I am not worth anything better and that work, and others were more important than I was.

My behaviours would back up my belief and I would reap that which I was sewing, the law of attraction, as you now know, returns to you what you tell it you believe or want. Furthermore, I was working with and for others, all of whom were very successful and fully knew and believed it, What I was putting out helped them to feel superior and what they put out subconsciously helped me and many of my colleagues, to feel inferior, the universe was therefore matching and consolidating effectively in order to bring balance to everyone's belief system simultaneously. With absolutely no ill feeling or bad intention to or from anyone involved this was just the law of attraction balancing the universe which is its job.

Please don't get me wrong, looking back I feel no resentment whatsoever, I have now forgiven myself for this time as I was not aware of what I believed about myself deep down, or what I was attracting and unconsciously asking for. It is a lesson, and I have taken from it the ability to now show myself more love and respect as a direct result, however, my dearest wish is that this experience and learning of mine, will assist many of you to consider, understand and make any necessary changes to your own lives much sooner than I did, in which case, it will make my lesson so much more worthwhile and help many others to benefit from that experience.

During the time that I took out of work, I found my true-life path and became a medium, which meant that

I belonged somewhere. I now had a purpose, fulfilling my desire to help others. Working on myself and banishing untrue beliefs, together with the subsequent positive affirmation work, meant that I reinstalled faith and value in who I was, and this started the process, enabling me to raise my own self-esteem and ultimately, I became important within my own world. The value that I placed on myself finally matched the value which I placed on others. Now that I had rebuilt me, I had to ensure that I would not allow myself to regress. I had to set boundaries.

This sounds simple; however, you must become very aware and conscious of what you are doing to yourself, what you allow others to do to you, and where a line needs to be drawn, it is not as easy as it sounds. I needed to look at my work ethos, my homelife, the balance between the two as well as what I did for others and how I was prepared to be treated.

I started with work, I was not expecting the shock that I uncovered. I knew that once I became self-employed, I was working too much, but I had never considered the impact of my ignorance. When I started this process, I was working with a client base of thirty-four learner drivers each week. This was fifty-two hours of actual tuition, plus half hour travelling time between lessons so I was working for seventy-eight hours and being paid for fifty-two of them. Considering fuel per week and maintaining the cars, basically I was working for less than half price.

I am no mathematician (clearly!) however, I was capable of the realisation that this did not make sense.

Don't get me wrong, the life of a driving instructor, being outside every day and meeting literally hundreds of people, all so very different and helping them learn such an important life skill is amazing, but someone with better business skills than I would have made it financially viable as well. It took me many years, but eventually, a further lesson learned.

The next area of my life to be looked at was my work life balance, as my pupil count reduced, I started spending more time working on my new interest in mediumship, ensuring weekly commitments to church and a circle and some time for me as I started to reintroduce my walking. I had always been musical as a child and certainly used to surround myself with music or radio all the time in my teens and early twenties but in retrospect, music seemed to disappear at about the same time as the fun in my life. Music returned to its rightful place along with a further uplift of my general mood as whilst I have never been a naturally miserable person, I had certainly become quite serious in my outlook, but, upon that realisation, immediate changes were made.

I moved on then to how I am treated by others. Having experienced unpleasant relationships and certainly the fear and lack of self-worth, which became an intrinsic part of my life, I can look back now, and whilst it was a difficult and on occasions horrific experience, it has shown me the importance of boundaries.

Boundaries which relate to personal relationships of any kind, not just heart based, are essential. They do not say anything about the other person, when correctly set, they say a huge amount about the respect and love that you have for yourself. By setting boundaries, not only do they establish the way others may treat you, but they make you very aware of how you should treat others too, in order to demonstrate the respect that you wish to be shown in return.

Boundaries are a tool essential for both the formation and the maintenance of equal interpersonal relationships, be it with a partner, friends and family, working relationships teacher/student, in fact all types. No matter what status each party holds in life, business etc, the base line is that we are all souls, humans, people, call us what you will, but no person has the right to treat another differently to the way in which they are, themselves prepared to be treated. One of my favourite analogies here is that irrespective of status or wealth, prince or pauper, our graves are all dug the same size.

I started by looking at what 'qualities' I had been drawn to with my two major relationships and realised how well they suited the unreal beliefs that I had previously held. They did not, however, serve me any longer. Today, what is important to me differs dramatically. I no longer have the need for a Strong, Alpha male to keep me in my place and render me helpless. Instead, I considered how I wanted to be treated now, this included equality, kindness, sensitivity, respect, love, support and understanding. (vastly different to my previous needs I think you will find!). I forgave myself for the previous mistakes and I forgave the people involved. As mentioned before, I never forgive the deed, that which is done, cannot be undone, but the lessons should be learned, however I forgave the individuals as I was no longer prepared to carry the regret for them. Whilst not easy it eventually removed that regret, the pain, together with the fear and sadness from my memories.

I no longer attract, or put myself in a position which would allow me to get close to anyone with the "qualities" that I used to unconsciously seek out, now, I look for the type of person with whom I feel comfortable and on a level with, when I socialise because by no longer mixing with people who would have previously drawn me to them, I know that when I finally decide to settle down, that I would have consciously attracted someone who deserves the love and support that I have to give and will need in return. It is also very important that we are together for the right reasons. I will have consciously considered what I bring to them, and what they bring to me on both an emotional and a practical level. This may, on first impression feel a bit cold and tough, however, my boundaries are there because I both love and respect myself, therefore any potential partner will need to feel the same about me, and, I would hope, about themselves too. I now have a set of work and personal boundaries which protect me and prove that I now hold the same regard for myself that I would afford anyone else.

Chapter 10
Find the foundation.

This is the point in the book where you can start to learn to use the various techniques and "mash ups" which really worked for me. I will describe, stage by stage what I did and how you can do it.

Wherever you have a belief about yourself or the world it is you, or more correctly, your subconscious mind, that has placed it there. Our own belief system starts "learning about life and the world around us" from within the womb, our consciousness starts to take effect at about two months prior to birth and is at its most active until we are approximately seven years old when it starts to settle down a bit.

Until then, pretty much everything that happens to us is new, but, by about the age of seven, we have established a fairly solid foundation of beliefs about our world. As a result, we have formed the majority of our initial basic belief system. Each time one of these beliefs are triggered by a similar experience, the mind takes the new scenario and compares it to what it already "knows". If this new scenario matches a previous belief, it is accepted, if it does not then the mind rejects what we are trying to do as unsafe, this is a protection mechanism and you will recognise this by that strange sense of uncertainty and foreboding that you feel deep in your gut sometimes. when doing something completely new. If we force the new scenario, and it proves safe, once repeated a few times, we have new learning which will either set a new belief or alter that which had previously been established. These are then consolidated or challenged by the nature of our environment or the nurture and teachings of those around us.

I personally found it hard to believe that learning could take place before birth, however, one day, during a professional workshop session, I was working with another therapist and I felt an emotion of intense fear, seemingly out of nowhere, so we went with it and suddenly, the forty something year old me was sitting on a chair, sobbing, with my arms pulled tight to my chest and I was bent down towards my knees.

I was holding my breath and the facilitator came flying over and repeatedly told me to breathe, but I couldn't, so she quickly almost screamed at me "how old are you?" and to this day, I do not know where this came from, because it did not even feel like inside, but I said, "I am being born", she immediately asked "what's happening"? and my answer was "I can't breathe, I am not moving". Her next question to me was "right now, what do you feel about yourself or the world?" my reply was so immediate, that she had barely said "the world" before I answered. "I am stuck, I am not safe and there is nothing I can do."

Immediately, I could breathe again, as if nothing had happened. This had shocked me and my peers and quite worried the facilitator for a bit, because of my physical responses, i.e. I literally stopped breathing and assumed an almost foetal position, and the words, were so precise, so immediate and completely without thought, it was like I was watching and listening to someone else. I later asked my Mum if there were any issues during my birth and she said no, so my consciousness had clearly picked up a moment between contractions when my system wanted to start breathing but I hadn't quite been born, however one of my earliest beliefs was formed right at that moment.

 I had absolutely no idea about holding this belief, because nothing, to my knowledge at that time, had ever triggered such a feeling, or so I thought. Neither did I even realise that it was possible for such a rational thought process, even before birth. On reflection, I realised, that at the time that we did this workshop, I was about eighteen months into the abusive relationship and regularly got extremely frightened. When he would start to shout and throw things I always held my breath, recoiled almost into a ball with my arms held tight into my body (although I never realised it at the time, I had always adopted an almost foetal-like position) until he stormed off. I was frozen, powerless and fearful of getting hurt, furthermore I knew I had no strength to change the situation and that I was stuck there. So, something inside of me, used this workshop to try and alert me to the reason that I had not got out of the "relationship". Even though he lived in my house, rent free, it was because of a belief I had been running since before I was born. The belief that I was stuck and could do nothing was backed up by the belief that I was powerless and out of control which came from a riding accident when I was 23, so you can see how powerful these apparently unrelated subconscious beliefs are, how they build and merge to "protect" us and the subsequent control they have over us and yet, we remain ignorant of their existence unless we are specifically looking for them.

Beliefs can be newly formed, or they can be as old (or, as in my case a few minutes older), than you. Our job is to find any that are having a negative effect on us. I have mentioned previously that many memories are repressed for our own protection, however when we go looking for them, deliberately, with healing in mind, you will be surprised how, in the correct environment they can surface very quickly and often with some extremely strong emotions attached. Be prepared, have tissues, and once they are out it is an idea if you are able, to immediately write down the feeling, the number colour age etc and the exact words of the belief that you are running if you get them at the time, as this will make working on the belief much easier if you are quoting its content word for word.

Very occasionally, as I touched on before, something is deemed by the mind to be very dangerous for you to be consciously aware of, and therefore it is repressed so deeply, that you are blocked from finding it, if this is the case, you will know that certain situations continually cause a very out of context emotional response. Try the methods here, but, if they do not produce answers that you can work with, seek a professional therapist to help you.

In many cases, once you have uncovered the detail that forms the foundation of your belief, you wonder why it is such an issue, however, bear in mind that if you formed a belief as four year old child, for example, your body stores the severity of that incident based on the perspective of the child, it does not mature with age, it is like a splinter of you that detaches itself and is suspended right at that moment. In cases such as these, sometimes just looking at the whole situation from an adult's perspective now, forgiving yourself or any other person involved may be enough, in order to remove the emotion from the memory, and it can, then be re-filed, however, if it was a traumatic event work through the belief based on the method described in chapter thirteen later, and if necessary use some inner child work as described in chapter fifteen.

If, what you find is that you just believe something negative about yourself and there is no particular memory that started it, and no apparent reason for that negativity, then positive affirmation is going to be the way to alter how you feel about yourself. Whichever way you need to work on this, please remember why you have uncovered this, what effect, holding this belief or negativity towards yourself, is having on you, and realise that you are in complete control. You can, should you choose, carry on feeling miserable and accept it, or you can make the decision to change it and if you do then you need to really commit to seeing this through.

If you do, and if you believe that you are more than worth it, then you can make significant changes to you, your life and your future, as well as the world around you. I have done it myself, I have helped clients and given them the tools to continue to help improve their lives and subsequently seen the results for myself. I have also worked casually with friends and family. I promise you that if you have the right attitude, commitment and put in sufficient effort, you will, without a doubt, get the results that you need, and you will see and feel the change for yourself.

We will start by finding out if there is, in fact, an unreal belief affecting you. If so it will be identified by correct use of the questioning technique detailed later, to unearth what decision(s) you made, about yourself or the world at the precise moment, a significant event happened. When you find the memory of the event or situation that first triggered the belief, you will have found the foundation of that belief, as well as the emotions and thoughts which accompany it. Once this foundation is located and destroyed, everything that that it has been supporting has to collapse, all the negativity, fear, pain or limits that have been imposed on you will be gone. This is your opportunity to bury them and use positive affirmations or conscious behavioural changes to re-define yourself and make the most of your new freedom.

Depending on the memory itself, we will then go on to use one or more, from a mix of techniques to remove it, where necessary replacing any limiting belief, which we have removed, with a positive one using an affirmation. This process will allow the memory to be re-filed as a known event but with any painful or emotional trigger taken away. Bear in mind that initially you may be unaware of the precise detail of the event because it may have been repressed for your own sake at the time that it happened. Do not worry if this is the case, if you can get a belief or an emotion, even without much detail, then you will be able to clear it.

It may even be the case that awareness alone, will play a role. Once you locate the foundation for a belief or behaviour which does not serve you well, due to the different frame of mind with which you now see that event, you may be able to recognise some learning that came from it. It may have been a life lesson which you can now understand, and even see what good you took from that particular situation. If so, the only healing necessary might be forgiveness which, if it comes absolutely from your heart with the correct intention, can often be sufficient to let go of the pain surrounding an unpleasant memory.

You may recall that once I had removed the beliefs that I had been running, during the years that I spent in an abusive environment, I continued to beat myself up for allowing such treatment, however, I consciously forgave myself for being weak due to the situation and the beliefs that I had subsequently found, and I forgave him, because of his lack of social skills. Because I did this very formally and absolutely from my heart it felt final. All the pain was immediately removed from the memory and it has never returned. For all that I experienced during that time, I can honestly say that because I was not prepared to carry his guilt for him, understanding my own learning and forgiving him, and more importantly, myself, has given me complete peace.

The very first step is to establish what is making you feel that something is not quite right. It may be obvious, for example, in certain situations you may consistently be dramatically over reacting, you may get upset, you may get inappropriately angry, or you may get violent for what seems to be no apparent reason. For me, I had experienced two relationships, one wasn't great and the second was horrible. I knew that I had lost my confidence, my personality was changing and that I no longer had fun, I also knew that I was getting very serious, I could find no reason to laugh even when others did, but I was crying regularly, alone in the car, in the bath, pretty much whenever I felt safe enough. I was very aware why I was upset, but I knew that there had to be a reason that caused me to go from one bad relationship to another, because of course, there is no such thing in life as a coincidence!

I hope that by now you understand that the foundation to any belief that you are carrying is buried deep within your subconscious mind and as such will take quite some unearthing. The only way to find these intrusive little mites, is to relax yourself sufficiently that your conscious mind, the one which registers what you are seeing, saying, doing, and generally deals with immediate thoughts, takes a back seat, because then, you are working within your subconscious mind. In this way you are dealing directly with the programs which are running you.

There are a couple of ways of achieving this. The first way is to establish the sort of mind state that you need in order to go into meditation, this will slow your breathing down and bring your energy down a little, this is nothing to be frightened of, you are doing nothing different to the process you use when you start to daydream, or the way you feel just as you are going to sleep or just waking up. You will have a slower brainwave pattern and your conscious mind says to itself "ok, nothing to do here" and takes a little rest. So, by doing a meditation and getting to that daydream place, you will be able to access your subconscious mind. You can't damage it, you cannot unconsciously program it whilst it is resting there is nothing to worry about.

The other way of doing this is with your breathing alone, sitting comfortably in a safe place, close your eyes and slow your breathing down a little, make each in breath slower and deeper than the last and push each breath out more deliberately than the last so that you draw in lots of air and push the air out, on exhalation you will feel your mind slowing and your body relaxing. Whilst you are in this gentle, relaxed state you need to answer a series of questions in a quickfire way. If you can have a friend or family member who can ask the questions it will be much easier, if not you can have the questions written down and write down the first word that comes to your mind, do not stop to think what the right answer might be, that will re-engage your conscious mind and you will think about your answer, this is not what we want. So, for example, if the question is "what day is it and the first thing that comes to your mind is a pink elephant, that is the correct answer

First, you need to think about what is troubling you briefly, say for example it is that you feel on edge whenever you are in a busy shop, imagine, or visualise yourself in a busy shop, now double the amount of people, do this again and again until you can feel your anxiety build, once you connect with that anxiety, very quickly answer these questions: (the first few just get you into answering quickly without thinking)

What is your first name?

What colour is your hair
What colour are your eyes
How old are you
What is
your favourite pet's name
Do you drive
Do you work?
What is your job title?
What was your favourite school subject
What is your favourite hobby
Give me a shape
Give me a colour
Solid, liquid or gas
Give me a number
Is that years old or years ago
Give me a feeling/emotion

The initial questions to get you going can be pretty much anything that you know on immediate recall.

I cannot stress enough that you must not think of an answer, if you say, "err…um…. orange" what you have done is brought yourself back to the conscious, rational mind and you will say what you think you should, not what you need to. You will never be able to locate a belief when your conscious mind is active.

My starting point was to try and find why I was attracting bad relationships, so I replayed, in my mind, few of the abusive situations that made me so fearful, until I felt upset and anxious, here are my questions and answers:

What is your first name? Victoria
How old are you? 47
What colour is your hair? Brown

What colour is your car: Blue
Who is your best friend: Karen
Who was your first teacher: Miss Cole
What is your favourite pets name: Monty
Give me a shape: Square
Give me a colour: Blue
Give me a number:2
2 years ago, or age 2? Age 2
The blue square is it solid, liquid or gas? Solid
How did you feel when you were 2? Lonely, isolated
What decision did you make about you or the world at
that moment? I'm not important.

So, I had a solid blue square at age 2 I felt lonely and
isolated and I was not important.
I have already mentioned this session earlier in the
book, so I will be brief here with what you already
know. My solid blue square was my family, once I
realised when it was, I immediately knew what it was, it
was that my Mum would have been nursing my brother,
so I got less attention at that time, but the belief that
the 2-year-old me made on that day would have
"proved" true every single day for quite a while so the
belief was formed and consolidated.
The memories that I do have of my childhood are
extremely happy, and I have always loved my brother to
bits, so there was no indication to anyone, myself
included that any belief existed, I did not get jealous or
naughty but my subconscious filed it as a known fact (a
belief).

On reflection, the only thing that does come to my
mind now, is that at school I was quite a loner, if I had
friends they were good friends, but I only ever had one

or two at a time and was much more confident of myself, when I was around animals than people. This was not to extreme in any way and neither I nor anyone else ever thought twice about this. I was just an animal lover. However, animals of course, must look to humans for everything in their world, so because I cared for them, I was important to them and that would have given me, something that subconsciously I felt that I was missing. This explains why I bonded with animals much more quickly than I did with my peers.

As I grew up I became more sociable, however, these deeply held beliefs will look to draw us towards situations which match what is "known" to the subconscious, so I was naturally attracted to men who confirmed my belief that I was not important, and there should be someone else who was more important than me. (one was separated from his wife, he was totally open and honest and had adult children, all of whom, quite rightly came first and the other, (I eventually found out) had an ex-girlfriend who remained in his life and he saw her several times a week throughout the time that he was with me. (She and his own family were told that he rented a room, so to the outside world I never even existed). As you can see, my subconscious brain was doing the most amazing job of matching its belief. Although the realisation of this did initially upset me, once I had removed the belief I could at least look back and know that it wasn't my bad taste in men or me having bad luck or life being cruel, it was just nature doing what it is supposed to, and I have found it easy to forgive myself and them and I have learned to be grateful for the many important lessons learned.

Before I started to run through the questions I got into a very relaxed state, (chapter twenty-one will introduce you to meditation and how to relax your mind). I did not think about any answers at all until I turned the paper over and they all came quickly, even the belief and, if you stay in the correct part of the brain, you will find the same. If someone does not immediately know the belief that they formed it is because they are back to the conscious brain but as long as you have a shape, a colour and a number you can carry on and get to the belief or even work through it without, a bit later. This is a very straight forward situation. I was able to locate an age, what was happening to me at the time how I felt, what it made me believe and why.

If you or the person that you are helping are in the correct mind, as in very relaxed and not trying to think about your answers then you can always get to a colour, a shape and a number as you literally want the first colour, shape or number that comes to mind. The belief, if not known immediately, should be easy to find as the person involved will know what was happening in their life at the stated age. By re-framing what you are looking for you can isolate the time of your life.

If you got a green triangle, mist or gas, which made you frightened and a number 4, and established that it was age 4, you would ask yourself, 'What, at the age of 4, involved a unit of 3, outside and made me feel frightened, like everything was closing in on me?' this could, for example, be that your parents took you to a big city for an outdoor event where there were thousands of people and the crowds were massive. A happy family day out for all intents and purposes, but to a 4 year old little person, that could have been very frightening, being in the centre of a crowd of big gown ups that you didn't know and may have resulted in fear, claustrophobia, or anxiety in crowds, or a fear of being shut in an unknown area, without knowledge of exits, but you would not ever have considered it as a trigger, because all you "know" is that when you were 4, for example, you went and watched Charles and Diana go past on the day they got married.

Sometimes, when we feel that something is not as it should be, we look for a reason but can't find anything specific that may have instigated a change in our emotional state. This can often mean that it is a damaged or under developed confidence or strength. If so, this would generally be confirmed by the person naturally displaying low self-esteem or a recent loss of self-esteem. Alternatively, the person becomes or has always been uncomfortable in one or two specific situations. If you are certain that the questioning technique bought up no strange or irrational beliefs which need to be removed, then regular and committed positive affirmation work, will improve the feeling of self-worth, leading to a happier demeanour.

Alternatively, if you are looking for, but not finding, an emotional belief but know that your behaviour or response to certain situations has changed, then either, you are not relaxed enough to be working completely in your subconscious mind, or, you tried to think of an answer which pulled the conscious mind back to the fore. If this has happened because you were writing the answers down, then you may find it easier to do a full meditation and turn to your questions at the end whilst you are still in a meditative state and/or request the help of a friend or family member to ask the questions very quickly in order that you have no time to think.

Once you know the belief and have identified whether it is recent circumstances that have created it, like my beliefs of being pathetic and ridiculous, which had been created in my forties because I was consistently told this by another, then positive affirmations are generally what will replace this irrational belief. If, however, they have been installed for many years, then the visualisation technique will be the way to go. You will find information further on about colours and shapes etc. and how to interpret them towards the end of the book.

Chapter 11
Use the eyes of another

This is a very traditional method to be using during any therapy which deals with lack of confidence, low self-esteem or where unreal and/or limiting beliefs are controlling a person's ability to move forward in life, or indeed, they feel that they are in fact moving backwards. Once you know that something negative is getting in your way then you need to find what it is. The next step then is to locate the belief as we covered in chapter ten, once you have found it, you need to decide whether it is true, which can be easier said than done if your confidence has been knocked for six, so this is our first visualisation practice.

You need to find a safe, quiet place and time where you know that you will not be disturbed. It can be useful to have a mirror nearby, but it is not essential. Close your eyes, and clear your mind, taking several deep, slow breaths in, and out to settle you. Now imagine yourself standing on your own initially, somewhere you are comfortable, so for example, your bedroom or lounge. Now, take a look at (or think through) you standing there. Next, I want you to imagine someone who you love, absolutely and who you respect, as a person who loves you unconditionally, a partner, parent, a child, family member or best friend, someone with whom you are always yourself, no pretence, you can just be you and they would always be honest with you.

Now imagine yourself, stepping out of your own body and into that of the other person. See through their eyes, hear through their ears, think with their mind and feel with their heart – not yours. Picture the person that you are "using" and think about their qualities, their very best traits, and why you chose them. This will generally be that you trust them, like them and they are popular so that many other people value their opinion, something like this puts you into a positive mind frame. See the world as they would through their eyes, feel confident inside, you are no longer you, open your eyes and look in the mirror or imagine looking at you. See yourself, but as **they** would see you, think their thoughts and really look honestly at yourself then tell yourself exactly what they, positively feel or recognise about you, list every good trait, deed, manner, everything – don't be shy, it's important to get everything possible out, spoken and ideally written down. Repeat this visualisation of them telling you the good things that they see in you, several times and accept them graciously. Do not diss or refuse them, honour what the other person thinks, it is their opinion, not yours. Finally, hold onto the love they have for you and imagine yourself stepping back out of their body and back into your own, but taking with you all the positive and happy thoughts that they would feel.

Now, have a look at what "they" said and how they felt and look at the belief that you have previously established inside. Taking any personal feelings away **look only at the facts** – is your belief true? No. It is only you that thinks this way, so, you now know that you need to work on **you**. You need to remove the belief, forgive yourself and any other party involved, and if necessary replace what you have removed with a positive belief by way of an affirmation, which is, in fact true and matches what those who love you know to be real.

As an example, when I did this, myself, I stepped into my Mum, she has always said about me that she admires my ability to roll my sleeves up in a crisis and work through it, I listed the honest facts that she would immediately state, these included my work ethic, the best side of my personality, the fact that I have my own home, that I have set up and run my own business, my ability to work independently, and as part of a team. At the time that I did this exercise, I had been convinced by repetition that I was useless, pathetic and had no value so these two opinions of me were worlds apart. I could not argue my "mum's words" because these facts were known by me to be true, and I certainly valued my mum's opinion most, however, years of the constant snide comments, put downs and bullying had buried what I had known, and I had installed the negative beliefs.

It was clear to see how I had been "taught" these new feelings about myself and once I realised how much damage this had done to myself unconsciously, and to my self-esteem, I was able to work on the emotions that were attached to these unreal beliefs. I then created a positive affirmation and repeated it many times a day for a couple of months or so, until a new, positive and honest belief was installed.

Chapter 12
Positive affirmations:

Once a limiting or unreal belief has been found and removed, then it is time to replace it. The important thing about positive affirmations is that they must be used many, many times in order to form the new belief. If you think about it we listen to our parents talking all day, every day, for months before we give it a go, and walking also takes a very long time, so learning occurs due to practice and repetition, lots and lots of repetition. You are looking to create a short phrase, ideally just one or two sentences, that you find easy to memorise. Once created, in order for it to work, you must commit to repeating this phrase as many times a day as you can, and this needs to be every single day. When you can, say your affirmation in front of a mirror it is stronger because you are looking at yourself at the same time as you are telling yourself. So, if you can, use a mirror first thing in the morning and last thing before you go to bed, and use the affirmation many more times a day in between, then you really will be giving yourself, the very best chance, of this new belief becoming part of who you are, as quickly as possible.

Initially, it will feel embarrassing, unbelievable, weird or difficult to say with real sincerity, however, stick with it, I guarantee that if you take the time and make the effort, there will, with continued practice, come a time that you absolutely believe its content, at this point don't stop. Keep going, it may take weeks or months. Once you can say it, believe it and you feel good about yourself at the same time, it will be something that you absolutely know, and you will have successfully installed a strong new belief. Once this forms part of what your subconscious mind knows to be true, you will start to notice your behaviours changing, what others see, will be a reflection of your new attitude. Your new behaviour, confidence and respect for who you are, will, as a result, continue to bolster your feelings of self-worth naturally.

 Here are some examples of one-line affirmations – use these phrases or adapt them to use the context in your own wording and you have made a great start,

Lack of confidence:
 I am a strong confident person and I love and respect myself.
 I am a strong, confident and capable person and I am learning and growing all the time.
 I trust myself, I believe in myself and I know that I am a strong and lovable person.
 I am a successful, confident person and I love and respect myself.
 I am strong, honest and reliable and I deserve the very best that this universe has to offer

Lack of self-worth:
 I am a kind and generous person, those who deserve my love are fortunate to have me around.
 I am a beautiful, loving, kind person, my friends value me and I absolutely value myself.
 I deserve a happy and fulfilling life and I am going to make sure that I get it
 I completely love and accept myself for who I am.
 I deeply and completely love and accept myself

I am a kind and generous person, I give my all and I deserve the very best of everything

Feelings of inadequacy or stupidity:
I am a strong, intelligent and beautiful person who deserves love and respect
I am proud and happy with the person that I have become and strive for continuous growth
I am a genuine and honest person who deserves love and respect from myself and those around me
I am intelligent, strong and capable of achieving anything that I put my mind to.
I am a happy, caring, intelligent person and I am growing all the time

Lack of love for yourself:
I totally and completely love and accept myself
I have shown strength through adversity and I am proud of all that I have achieved
I push myself to grow more every single day and it makes me happy and proud of myself
I am the strongest person that I know, and I love myself for that reason
I am an honest caring person and completely deserve love and respect from myself and those around me.

Feeling Ugly or different from others.
I am a beautiful person full of love for myself and the world around me.
I am a beautiful, strong person worthy of love from myself and others
I am intelligent, caring, beautiful and strong, I have pride in myself and all I do

My heart, my soul, my body and my personality are full of beauty, strength and love.

I am a beautiful, loving soul and I thoroughly deserve unlimited love and happiness from this kind and generous universe

Affirmations should be said clearly, slowly and deliberately, you want your subconscious mind to take them in. Even in the beginning, when it is difficult, say them as if you absolutely, completely and utterly mean every single word, ideally in front of a mirror, but many, many times a day right up until you go to sleep.

The law of attraction section will help you to better understand why, what you put out to the universe comes back to you and how your own thoughts and feelings about yourself and the world will completely affect how others see you as well as how you see yourself.

Chapter 13
Healing - a release for emotionally based beliefs.

The techniques that I will introduce to you here, are ones that I have adapted initially to work on myself, but then I have gone on to use very successfully with clients. My methods have their foundation in a mash up of counselling, hypnotherapy, Emotional Freedom therapy, mindfulness, and visualisation techniques. I have tweaked and mixed them up to get quick, hard hitting results for clients who have emotional and often irrational symptoms. These should only be used as tools for self-help when there are no underlying medical, psychiatric or acute conditions present.

The main method that I use, and adapt accordingly is a strong, tough and generally, quick way to work on a limiting or self-sabotaging belief. If you are able to keep an open heart and an open mind and be completely honest and true with yourself, then this has proved time and time again to be an extremely effective method which can produce some exceptional results. It does, however, exactly what it says ……. It releases emotion, and boy, have I experienced personally, and with clients some very dramatic emotional releases!!!

I mentioned earlier that even with my adaptations, I have, with clients and for myself, released some really stubborn blocks and I have experienced clients shouting, swearing and once, screaming, because they finally found a way to get what had been locked inside, often for years, out. I have also witnessed what I can only describe as projectile crying, sobbing so hard that breathing actually feels difficult. Please don't get me wrong, not everyone has such dramatic reactions, it depends on how negative the emotional event was, and how much damage has been done by it being supressed over the years, we are not setting out here to deliberately upset anyone, such reactions vary from person to person and are not as a response to the therapy, they are the way in which emotion gets released, by that particular individual, from the body, if an emotional situation has been supressed deep down for a long time but it is affecting your life, you will need quite some metaphorical "crowbar" to move it, this determines the force with which it is expelled.

"Better out than in", my Nan used to say about many things, but emotion was one of them. If we ignore it, we basically remove the pin and start the clock ticking on an emotional time bomb. Therefore, to release the emotion, and get it out there on the table, allows us to look at it with a fresh pair of eyes in a safe way. When we are ready, then we can deal with it for good and discharge it (a small, controlled explosion) and, if necessary, fill any vacuum left with a positive belief, then you have disarmed a very nasty enemy, taken control and made yourself very much stronger.

This will make way for more confidence, peace, and personal growth. If you have more than one belief, then to address them one by one and remove their control over you, will make a massive difference to the way you feel, the way you act, and life can only become very much better.This is something that I have experienced for myself, and I have seen clients change, literally before my eyes, in some cases when what we have released is something really big, which had been affecting them for years, they visibly appear younger when a very serious weight has been lifted.

At this point, before we look in any detail at the technique and it's use, I would like to dispel the myth:

Crying is not a sign of weakness.
Crying and releasing of emotion is not only a strength, it shows respect and self-love. An emotion supressed will find its way out, either catching you off guard, and bringing tears anyway, when you don't want them. Alternatively, it may find its own release in anger, violence, mood swings, depression, anxiety or manifest itself in either mental or physical illness, let me explain why.

When we all walked this earth as Cavemen and women we were designed to be nomadic and we were hunter/gatherers. As such our menfolk went out at first light to find and kill animals for meat for the tribe and went in groups for safety. Our good ladies were charged with childcare and finding berries, fruits etc, supplied by the land to accompany the meat and on days of a meagre or non-existent kill, instead of the meat.

Our creator, very kindly, equipped us with a handy tool. In order to give us an opportunity of survival during dangerous times, he provided us with what we refer to now, as our fight or flight mechanism. So, if you were out clubbing animals, or picking berries, and you parted the long grass in front of you, and found yourself in a tricky situation, perhaps face to face with a hungry lion, also out hunting, you have a fraction of a second to decide. 'Do I run like the bionic man or do I summon some super human strength from out of thin air and go for the kill first?'.

This fight or flight mechanism gives us the ability to make a snap decision and, if necessary, also the "super human out of thin air" ability to find speed or strength to run or stand and fight. It does so by releasing a chemical called adrenalin into the body, which acts as an immediate fuel injection and it is the subsequent running or fighting that ignites and uses up this adrenalin to clear the body of the toxin.

In modern times, we no longer, generally, find ourselves in such life-threatening situations, however, emotional pain, fear and anxiety, depression, and other extreme emotions, can cause the body to activate this pre-installed protection mechanism because, the brain registers stress. Adrenalin is produced into the body, in exactly the same way.

If the stress is ongoing, a further chemical, Cortisol is released which provides a longer-term stress control, however long term the body's internal balance cannot cope with these substances. These days, most of us tend not to fight or physically run away from our problems, so, these unused toxic substances, remain sloshing around inside us.

In small doses this is ok but in large doses this alteration to the body's internal.ph balance, causes dormant cells to flourish. We all have dormant cells, including cancer cells inside us but, by allowing the body to be constantly out of balance in this way, these dormant cells activate, causing undesirable health issues to arise, Cancers, heart attacks, depression, anxiety, and ulcers, to name but a few, can all be triggered initially, by us holding extreme amounts of emotion inside.

Many people get treated for critical illness such as cancers, heart attacks etc, and then, finally get the all clear, however, the human host, returns to their previous high stress lifestyle and make no change to the environment in which the illness originally thrived, so the cycle begins again.

Crying is our purpose-built mechanism to release emotion and it has a similar effect as running away or standing and fighting, it releases the emotion trapped within the body. Where people are bought up and conditioned that showing emotion is weak and they proceed to hold pain inside, the stress ultimately triggers the fight or flight reaction and stimulates adrenalin which the body cannot use. The chemical makeup of the body changes, and either the person releases the feeling, that the adrenalin produces with a reaction such as violence or anger, or the body gets out of sorts and depression, anxiety, mental or physical health disorders can occur.

By allowing or even, in the case of therapy, forcing the emotion out you are not only respecting this body that you have, and after all, we only ever have one, you are also removing some of the physical triggers of health-related conditions from later life. So, I stress here again, as I did earlier, showing and releasing emotion respects and honours yourself. It takes strength to put yourself first and look after your body. Weakness, I believe, is only in refusing to look after yourself and dealing with issues that will potentially place, both your physical and mental health at risk.

I will give you an example of a client who I worked with, she had started off as a driving school pupil, however, she seemed to have a habit of sabotaging absolutely anything that was going well in her life. Driving proved to be no exception. I could, however see that she was very capable of learning fairly quickly and I refused to let her give up, until we had tried to find any limiting beliefs that she might be running.

I was so convinced that we would find the answer quickly that I offered her a free therapy session and she begrudgingly agreed. We arranged some time for her to visit me with the aim of finding why she felt incapable of success. During our early discussions on the agreed date she told me that she had always struggled with her weight and had in fact had gastric band surgery many years ago, but the weight had pretty much all gone back on. She had also suffered with ulcers for most of her adult life, Furthermore, regarding acquisition of new skills, she assured me that it was nothing more than her inability to learn, it had been the same way with her adult education courses which she never finished, and her many attempts to get promoted at work (she worked in retail but had five attempts of stepping up a grade, had failed each and every time for different reasons and now given up).Using the questioning technique explained in chapter ten, we found very quickly that she was running a belief "I lose everything that is important to me" "everything gets taken away from me" she was completely unaware of having these thoughts consciously.

It transpired, with a little digging, that when she was in her early twenties, she had given birth to a baby boy, he was sadly, born very poorly, she never held him after delivery as he was rushed away to be worked on but could not be saved, he died before she ever met him. Everything was happening so quickly that she never dealt with it, but everyone said how strong she was for getting through the ordeal. The truth was, that she was in so much shock her body "protected" her, and the subconscious mind buried much of her emotion due to the fact that she had so many unpleasant things to deal with. She recalls being in a daze for about four months. She had never considered that this traumatic event would have caused other issues in her life, she was convinced that she had dealt with it and it was in the past, however once we had narrowed the underlying belief to his birth, I asked her what she thought when she remembered that event, although he was ill, what she had felt was they are "taking my baby away from me". At the time she had received extensive counselling which helped her greatly and she had assumed that everything had therefore been dealt with.

Her own Mother, who had been her rock, sadly passed away eighteen months later and when I asked her what her beliefs were after that she said, "everything important is taken away from me" and "I don't deserve love". The desire to give and receive love is one of the basic human givens, a necessity for us all, but that original thought led to her feeling that she was not good enough to be a mother otherwise the baby would have been ok. This thought process then further led to "I am not good enough" after her Mum passed away She had formed these beliefs after the death of her baby but did not realise that she needed further therapeutic help at that time. She explained that she had become "sloppy" as she put it, after she lost her mum, but she had just started to unconsciously act out what she felt about herself.

These new behaviours, after the passing of her mum, were the very same types of behaviours that I had witnessed in her driving, strong emotional outbursts, anger, frustration, and a strong propensity to just give up, try and get out of the car and walk away. It became apparent that as she felt that she had no control over that which she lost, she started unconsciously making mistakes at her promotion interviews, this was her subconscious mind initiating behaviour which backed up her belief that she was not good enough, and in an ironic way it took control of her situation by ensuring that she failed to get the promotion. The mind had succeeded as it matched the pre-installed belief.

During our conversations she mentioned that she was having the same problems with relationships and her constant dieting attempts. These actions further supported her feelings, matching a belief. She turned to comfort eating which served two purposes for her, firstly it felt good to eat, secondly the increasing weight gave her something to hide behind, and, in her mind, ensured that no man would look at her anyway, therefore, she could not ruin more relationships, nor could she cause another baby to die by getting pregnant again. She had treatment for two ulcers some years previously, which were put down to stress and it is clear to see why her body was crying out for help. Something had to give before the next "symptom" was a heart attack, cancer or severe mental health problems turned up

It was a very emotional session, we used the visualisation technique to reduce and remove the emotion from the memories, we had two more sessions to locate and eradicate additional secondary beliefs, both were for the purpose of just getting her to release the emotions held, and by the last of them she told me that she was not feeling anger inside any longer, she just felt tired and empty which was perfect, although she was emotionally void it was because she had finally released them. I sent her off, with a positive affirmation and to book some grief counselling as she was clearly still stuck within her grief

We restarted her driving three weeks later and she was already a different person. Her attitude was so dramatically changed, in fact she was so desperate to prove to herself that she was capable, that she had bought her own car for practice with her friend and as a result of all she had been through and the work she had done she excelled herself and passed her first driving test with only three minor driving errors. She told me that it was the very first time that she could remember doing anything successful and that she felt proud of herself.

This example is extreme, and this lady would not have been able to deal with this alone, my reason for sharing this with you is to demonstrate the effects of holding emotion inside. If you have a serious trauma like this you must seek help to deal with it, whether or not it is the cause of present day problems as the severity of that trauma was affecting all areas of her life, and her health, however the techniques we used will work for you if the underlying reason is serious but not traumatic and it will make a massive difference to your life if you give it a chance.

Chapter fourteen
The Visualisation Technique

Once you have found a belief that has control over you, i.e. it makes you behave in a certain way in a certain situation, you need to decide if this response is causing a positive or negative reaction. Sometimes it is clear to see that your actions when in a particular situation, stop you having the opportunity to do something that would be inappropriate or derogatory. However, if the response that you are showing in these scenarios does not protect or assist you and is, in fact, causing a negative response then the belief itself serves no positive purpose and needs to be removed.

Once the event or memory which caused the belief itself is located, then you will have a list of responses to the questions that were required. Potentially you may also have the belief wording itself. If, however, you were not able to ascertain the exact phrase, don't worry or guess as this may start you working on something that does not actually exist. Use exactly that information which you got when you were answering the questions and add nothing to your answers.

If it feels that you have insufficient answers, take yourself back into the emotion, really feel it deep inside and then with your eyes closed, take a number of very deep breaths both in and out, and quickly answer each of the questions again from scratch. Once you start the questions, remember that you do not need to use the initial basic answers such as your name or hair colour, as they are just to get you in the right mind space, however, it is essential to have the feeling or emotion, the colour, together with any additional detail that came to mind about the colour, the form, and the number (don't forget to establish whether that was years ago or years old).

With these answers you can narrow down the rough period of time at which the belief was formed. You may or may not have found the belief at this stage, however, you should be able to locate the situation, and, applied correctly, the process will, itself, provide what your mind needs. The age or time in your life and the colour and shape will provide a sufficient basis from which to start working on what was retained by your mind at the time.

I have encountered, with a couple of clients, situations where we worked on the picture they came up with based on a repressed memory which we never even managed to get into, however, we literally worked on the shape, the colour and the emotion that they felt, and we used a visualisation which seemed, at the time, irrelevant. (for example, one lady had a massive yellow circle, as big as the world, which we ultimately shrank to the size of a football and she literally visualised kicking it out of sight), however, in both cases the derogatory emotional reaction disappeared and never returned for or either client.

It is important to understand that our bodies and our minds communicate with us in a myriad of ways. Pain, emotions, intuition, psychic ability, energy changes, inexplicable thought patterns, thirst, hunger, or, when we absolutely ignore it, physical or mental health issues. Over the centuries we have generally grown to ignore such internal communication and we now go to doctors to tell us what is wrong physically, we go to therapists when we don't feel right emotionally, or we go psychics and card readers to tell us what, if we were to listen to it, our own intuition would in fact tell us.

That is why this system and others work. The body and mind will talk to you in metaphor so if I ask you to give me a shape that represents a bad feeling your mind will give you clues, a triangle means three people, things or situations, a circle – never ends, and so on.

The method

So, following the questioning you will have a colour, a shape, a number and an emotion, these are the important things.

The first thing to establish is the number let us say you got 5, then you need to know if it was age five or five years ago. Again, ask yourself without conscious thought – Let's say five years ago.

Then the colour and any description of the colour – let's say pink, pale pink

The shape – let's say a triangle – what does that triangle look like, again do not think – let's say an arrow

Then an emotion – let's say pain.

Then a belief, if you have one – let's say "it's all gone"

These were the exact answers that a lady gave me a few years ago, she had come to me for a mediumship reading but I felt a need was crying out for some healing, so I asked her if she would be prepared for me to do so and she agreed. This is what came out of it.

We had a pink triangle, five years previously, I asked her what her triangle looked like, it was an arrow, I said tell me about the arrow, she said it was very sharp, when she said sharp she suddenly got emotional, so I knew we were going somewhere with this. I asked her where she felt the pain and she put her hand straight to her chest. So, I asked her what had happened five years ago which pierced her heart. She immediately told me that she had lost a baby and as a result of the pain, she and her husband had a nasty falling out and ended up divorcing.

So, my lady and her husband, had been a close couple, and they got pregnant all was going well so here was our unit of three, then she lost the baby , she was very upset so there was no need to ask her when, but I had a feeling that it was quite a way into the term, then it got difficult for her to cope, and she said that she pushed her husband away because she could not handle the grief, so now she was on her own and distraught, she had indeed lost it all.

I asked her to visualise her pink triangle and describe it to me. She told me that it was massive, and she could not see under, over or round it. She was clearly stuck in the emotion and the memory, and the fact that she could not see past it meant that it was stopping her moving forwards. In essence, it was holding her stuck at the point in her past when she had two losses to deal with. Her pain was at a ten.

The pink was for the heart and the love, but I knew that the light pink meant something else to her and I could actually feel it from her, so I very quietly asked "did you give her a name", she found it difficult at first because she had never spoken to anyone in detail, because she was so grief stricken, no one could console her, or cope with talking to her. But she had named the baby and she spoke her name out loud for the first time. It was an emotional time. I asked her if she could imagine, what her daughter would be like now and she slowly started to tell me, how she felt she would look, and what her personality would be like. I asked her what her arrow looked like now, it was knee high and quite thin.

I asked her if she spoke to her daughter and she didn't, but I told her that she could, and should, because she was looking after her mum. Her pain was now at a two and the arrow was the size of a ruler, I explained to her that the arrow was the emotion and not her daughter, her little girl would always be with her in spirit. I asked her to imagine picking up the arrow and throw it as far away as she could, and she visualised herself throwing the arrow and it flew, in her own words "miles and miles" and way out of sight.

Because she had never dealt with the grief of losing the baby, or that of the separation she had locked the pain inside. Our visualisation and finally releasing the emotion, "throwing away" the pain and acknowledging her daughter had released the blockage, I asked her if she felt able to forgive herself as there was no specific reason for the loss, and therefore nothing that she could have done differently. she could, and she did. I asked if she could forgive her partner and she could as she finally became aware, that he too was grief stricken and I asked if she could forgive her daughter, she said there was nothing to forgive, I asked her what number the pain was at an she said she felt nothing, it was zero.

Next, I asked her to visualise herself, with her daughter as she would look now, and she could, I asked her to take the little girl's hand and imagine them somewhere lovely, she said the beach and described it to me. I asked her how she felt, she was really happy. So I asked her to take the picture, in her mind and make the colours as bright as possible, as strong as she could imagine, then blow the picture up until it touched the sky and went to the centre of the earth, she did, then I asked her to shrink the picture down to fit the palm of her hand, and finally to place her hand over her heart and let the picture melt into her heart so that she could always protect them both. This was an emotional release but something that my client was ready for an it was beautiful to see her finally find some peace with herself.

Hopefully you can see how we did this,
We got the questions, we found the event, we got a shape and knew it was sharp and exceptionally large to start with, we knew that the emotion was at a ten, we acknowledged the event by talking about the baby and bringing into our day by making her five and my lady described and spoke her name (what we did here was to bring her and her daughter forward as they were, in my client's memory, both stuck on the day that the baby died) all of a sudden the current pain she felt reduced, the obstacle, her big arrow was dramatically smaller, we discussed that it was ok for her to talk to her daughter and acknowledge her, then she "took hold of the pain and threw it away" Next she visualised the two of them holding hands on the beach which replaced her memory of the hospital as the last thing she saw. Finally, she made the picture so big, so bright, she could see nothing else, then she shrank it and placed it into her heart forever. We had removed the foundation and she could finally understand why she

and her partner split up and understood that neither could, at that time find a way to support the other and it came between them.

In essence it is a very simple technique and there are many much more complicated, but equally effective techniques which work exceptionally well in a therapeutic setting. All I did was to create a way that I could use this healing by myself. If you work from your heart, in love and with care, healing and kindness for yourself, you will not only be able to get the results, yourself, but you will get better at reading and deciphering them.

I have included more working examples of this method in operation below, and also in chapter twenty. These should help you to understand some of the different angles you can use to find and remove these emotional blockages for yourself. If you start making your body and mind important it will "talk" to you and, with practice you will start to hear it. I hope that you can now see this. You will find some tables at the back of the book which will give you the basic colours, shapes and forms and their usual meanings, however, we are individual so what you will find with practice, is that if you are working completely from your heart and keeping an open mind, then you, yourself, will start to get a feeling for what you are looking for and you may develop (or more correctly re-awaken) an inner "knowing" or your own intuition, call it what you will, but it is there already.

When you get to this stage then go with what it is that you feel inside, you will begin to realise what a colour means to you, for example a particular colour may mean one thing to you and another thing to someone else, you will eventually and with practice begin to understand the "language" of colour and interpret colours based on what they mean to you, it is perfectly possible for any human being to pick up psychic connections with the energy around them, be it your own or that of another person, the more that you come to listen to and understand your own inner guidance the more awareness and understanding that you will have of subtle changes in you and the world around you.

Looking from a different perspective (gut feeling)
For example, red would usually mean fear, anger or passion, but I worked with a young soldier once and he said red, however, these emotions did not **feel** to me that they fit him, I could not put my finger on it so to speak but my gut told me this was not what we were looking for. I decided to just ask him what was the first word that came to mind if he thought of the colour red. He immediately responded "poppies, remembrance" and I asked him what emotions he got when he thought of poppies, he told me sad, but proud as well. And I asked him what happened four years ago that made him both sad and proud, he said "Grandad never got to see me passing out". As a child, his father was not around, it was his Grandad who became the significant male role model for him during his early years, my client idolised him and it was grandad who inspired him to join up.

We located a belief that "he would "never get it quite right" He had spent most of his college years, just missing the grades he wanted, they were always ok and what he needed, but were a little shy of the results he expected of himself. His Grandfather had passed away when he was at high school, an original belief had been formed at that time, because the man he looked up to most in his life had literally, "left his world".The belief that "something important is missing" formed, naturally as a result of the grief that he felt, however, during high school and college his grades demonstrated to him that he "never quite got it right" which backed up that "something was missing". He was totally unaware of either belief, let alone any effect this may have had on the teenager himself.

These two beliefs, working hand in hand, were playing a significant role in creating his struggles through school, college and beyond. He was in fact, manifesting his own results to back up the beliefs. Unconsciously, setting his own bar so high that he could not possibly reach it, served to ensure that he never quite made the grade he wanted, thus proving to himself, that there would always be something missing.

We used a visualisation of him standing in front of a huge red door, I asked him to mentally ask his Grandad to come to stand beside him and bring the key for the door, I asked him if he could visualise this, and he could. I asked him to hug his grandad in his mind's eye and to follow the gentleman to the door which his grandad unlocked for him. Next, I asked him to step through the door first and turn and watch his grandad emerge then lock the door behind them. The door led them out to the parade ground on the day he passed out and he watched the scene with his grandad by his side. Whilst it was very emotional we had passed through the red door and he had a memory of his grandad standing with him and watching him on that special day. When I asked him to turn to his Grandad and describe how he looked, he said, "proud as punch" We started with sadness at a 9 and pride at a 4. When I asked him where the sadness was when they stood together, he smiled and said, "there is none, because he was there", I asked where his pride was now, out of ten and he beamed and said 100.

The beauty of working in this way is that where your conscious mind sees through your eyes, the subconscious mind cannot differentiate between thought and reality. The subconscious simply learns patterns that you experience, then wants to match them. As long as your visualisation, be it by seeing in your mind's eye or imagining yourself in that situation, contains all the detail you can possibly add, then the new picture is filed by the brain as just a more recent "memory".

This is the reason why, when I am working with a client who is visualising an event, I will get them to make the colours stronger and brighter, the picture grows up to the sky and down to the centre of the earth. I always then finish with shrinking it back down to fit in the palm of your hand and placing that hand over your heart and imagine the image melting into your heart where it stays protected and loved by you.

Another way of looking at it (this is for illustration purposes, not a case study)
Let us suggest that you have come up with:
Colour blue
Form solid

Shape triangle
Age 7
Feeling. alone
And as yet no belief.

The first thing is to consider is does something immediately come to your mind based on the age, for example, oh yes at seven we had a blue car and when Mum, Nan and I were out one day I was playing and accidentally locked the car whilst I was still in it with the keys inside. This may have caused Mum and Nan on the outside to panic and shout at you because you could not work out how to open the door.

Alternatively, at age seven you may have been at the beach and playing with your two older siblings who buried you in the sand up to your neck and ran away, it might only have been a couple of minutes until they returned but the seven-year-old would have felt alone and scared and frightened being close to the see and unable to move.

The colour: Blue can mean healing (needed or to be given), it can mean water, or it can mean air, it can be more literal, it may have made you feel blue (sad)or that something as in an object was blue, so keep an open mind and write the answers down perhaps in a circle so there is no definite order.

Consider all the options at the same time and one will feel right.

Another example from my client work:
Colour: Dark pink
Emotion: sadness
Shape: square
Form: fabric – like a sheet

Belief: It is my fault

12 years ago

Pink relates to the heart or love, so I asked my client what, 12 years ago made her sad deep in her heart she worked it back and she had been in her front garden with her younger brother and he had opened the gate (which was square) and their dog had run into the road and been run over. The lady had felt she was to blame as she was older and so should have been "in charge." The curtain related to the blanket they put the dog in to take it to the vets. The dog was not badly hurt but her subconscious had stored the dog got out when "I was supposed to be looking after everyone "We located a belief that "It's my fault". She had over the last 12 years, since the event slowly had her confidence reduced as she kept attracting things for which she felt that she was to blame so if anything went wrong, whether or not it was her fault, she assumed the blame and this had been continually consolidating her belief until she was literally acting as though if she did anything at all in life, she would make it fail or go wrong or in some way sabotage anything she was doing. The visualisation technique worked well for this lady. Her dark pink square was fabric in her visualisation of it, so we shrank it by looking from an adult perspective and she folded it up and put it in a bin, walked through the gate which she shut behind her to ensure it was closed and walked away until she could no longer see it.

As I mentioned before, you will start to get the feel for working in this way and you will eventually stop referring to the lists in this book, because if you listen to that little voice inside of you,(the one that says this doesn't feel right, or I bet that's Jane on the phone and then it is) we call it intuition, inner knowledge, sixth sense, call it what you will, but that little voice will say to you, blue means sad, red means excitement etc, you will actually realise that you can, personally interpret the responses that you are giving because they relate directly to how you would interpret them. When this starts happening go with it, the more that you practice, the more you will start to "feel" where the information that you get is coming from inside, this is how we can all tune into our own bodies. When you get really good you start tuning into people that you know or meet.

Any scientist that you talk to, will tell you that absolutely everything in this universe, you included, is made up simply of energy. It is only the particular frequency at which the energy moves that makes it look different, so as energy ourselves, we have a built-in ability to read energy, that is to say, pick up on thoughts, feelings etc of others. We get so bogged down with our everyday life and living in the past or future that we lose the sensitivity for this to be a natural occurrence, but it is there and the more work that you do of this nature the more you will start to "feel" energy again.

Twins have a shared energy and can read each other's mind from miles away because their energetic connection is so strong You are just tuning into an energy vibration – yours or someone else's.

Once you have located a belief which is subconscious but is having a derogatory effect on you and you have pinned it down to an age and found out what memory or event created that belief, then you need to work on it. The colour that you came up with is important so get as much information as you can so if it is red, what type of red, scarlet, pillar box, maroon, bright etc. find the shape, and find out any other information that your mind offers you, regarding the shape, so if you had a square , still in the subconscious part of your brain, ask yourself how big is it, what does it resemble, i.e. a wall, a wrapped gift, a large box, something like that, you may see it or just get the word straight into your head. Then find a form – so solid, transparent, liquid, thick or flowing, mist – thick like a heavy fog or wispy like a cloud.

An illustration of this.
Colour Grey
What type of grey: dark, dirty
Form – solid -like a wall
Shape – square
How big? Like a room
Are you in it or outside it?
Inside
This is sounding like someone feels trapped by an emotion – it has a form like a concrete wall – so in this case I would ask them if there is a door, if it is locked, ask them to see themselves look in their pockets (if they have trapped themselves in this belief – they will **always** have the key to release themselves and their subconscious will let them see it or feel it). If there is no door or no key their mind is telling them that they have **been** trapped, by the memory and not trapped themselves, so I would ask them to envisage, in the corner of the room, a large sledge hammer, and get them to picture themselves smashing a hole big enough to crawl through to the other side then walk away ten paces at a time, keep looking back until it is out of sight

(the ten paces gives a good bit of distance and they are walking consciously away from that which trapped them).

So metaphorically they had the belief, they have let themselves out if they had the key or smashed their way out if they were so trapped that they had no key then they have walked away from it.

Other uses for this technique

This technique can not only be used to work through a traumatic event, but if you have a fear or phobia you can use this to do what we call future pacing. This means tricking your brain by installing a memory (which was never there) in order to give it a successful pattern to match.

I have used this many, many times with driving school pupils who were petrified of, or have previously failed a test, be it practical or theory. I make them visualise arriving at whichever test centre they will be using (if it is a first time, I would show them round the test centre myself for a practical test), then get them to imagine turning up on the day, imagine being shown to a seat for theory or if it is a practical test, the examiner coming out and calling their name, them shaking hands and saying hello, then I talk them step by step through what will happen and we finish off with them finishing the test and being presented with the pass certificate.

I get them to do this with me a few times then practice with all the detail included as often as they possibly can prior to the test. The more you practice this visualisation, the more "memories" the brain has of passing a test so the more often it has already matched the pattern itself before the big day.

I have also used this with students who need help for taking GCSEs, 'A' levels or preparing for degree papers or even writing a dissertation. The success rates are fantastic, and fear is reduced dramatically if not eradicated completely as the subconscious brain has a pattern stored of "memories" of you previously passing this exam or test which it now strives to match.

You could use this yourself to practice public speaking, your wedding, anything that you are nervous about. The essential part of making this work is all the detail, the colours (make them bright, bold, completely vivid, other people who might be there, and if you can, visit the venue so it will be familiar to you, then practice this visualisation as often as you possibly can in advance. If you get lazy and do it once or twice, it is not installed as strong a belief but if you commit to this 100% you give yourself the very best opportunity of achieving the results that you want.

Don't forget what we covered in the law of attraction section. The universe wants to balance itself so if you keep visualising your success, you will believe it and the universe will give it back to you.

Chapter fifteen
Inner Child Work

When we go looking for beliefs, by the very nature of what it is that we are doing, we do not often know initially exactly where the memories, that created the beliefs themselves originated from. When you have located the memory, it could be reasonably recent, or it could stem from a situation which happened during childhood.

The more recently that the belief was formed can, sometimes, make it easier to shift because it can be rationalised by an adult brain. The fact that it has been in place for less time will help as well. However, an incident which happened to a child, can form some of the strongest beliefs and those which can take more to overwrite. Firstly, they have been in place for the longest, secondly, they have had the opportunity for that belief to be consolidated more often and of course ultimately, the effect of that situation happening to a child in comparison to an adult can be very dramatic.

When you are little, you have to trust grown-ups and that they would never hurt you or allow a situation to hurt you, and because of the sheer difference of having to look up at everything around you, due to your own size, almost everything in the world that is external to you will seem bigger than you and cause you to feel vulnerable. The trigger memory may be a repressed, serious situation, or it can be something which the adult, sees as insignificant, however, to the child, it can seem magnified, and potentially much more dramatic than it actually was.

When a belief springs from such a memory, it can again be dealt with, using a very similar visualisation technique. What we need to remember is that the memory was formed by the child, with a child's brain, so we must honour and heal the child and not the adult. This can be extremely powerful, and I have facilitated some very dramatic healing results for people who come to me with fears, phobias, or habitual patterns, the foundations of which are buried in childhood memories.

Again, I would urge you to seek professional therapeutic assistance if you have, or uncover, extremely traumatic memories, in order to ensure that you are fully supported throughout the process. If, however, you are looking to clear an emotional block or response which you find has been created during your early years this visualisation can work extremely well.

Always start with establishing the belief using the questioning technique demonstrated earlier. Once the memory of the event has been established, and the belief located, then you can set about working on it. If it relates to a straightforward situation, which you can now rationalise and are able to forgive yourself, as well as anyone else involved, then this forgiveness, used with a positive affirmation may be all that is required. If it is a nasty situation, but you understand that it could, and would not happen again, maybe because you have learned a lesson from it, or you are certain that you would recognise something similar, and not allow it to happen again, then to remove the underlying emotional effects, using the basic visualisation technique, should remove the foundation of any belief that was formed.

If, however, the belief was formed whilst you were a child, and the belief itself, is based around you or your environment not being safe, you feeling vulnerable, frightened or incapable of escaping that situation, then I would recommend doing some inner child work.

This is another visualisation. The difference is that you visualise the memory of what happened, in the form of a spectator, see the child at that age, frightened, upset or whatever emotional state you were in at the time, then place yourself into the visualisation as the adult that you are now. See yourself going towards the child providing them with comfort, safety and protection. You and only you will know how that child version of you would have wanted this comfort. If you are tactile then pick that child up and cuddle them tell them that they are safe, that you will never allow anything like that to happen to them again, and that you will always love and protect them from this day forward, If you are not so tactile you may see yourself sitting down next to them and saying the same thing. It is essential that the child you, knows and believes that you can and will protect them, and more importantly, tell the child that it was not their fault, you forgive them for being made to think that it was, you also forgive any other party involved, because they were incapable of doing better, or being a better person and you also must forgive yourself, as the adult, for anything that you may have felt, thought said or done in the time since the incident.

Next in your mind, take that child out of the place they were in to somewhere lovely, like a park, or the seaside, round the Christmas tree from your youth, or somewhere that you as a child would have been most happy. Then look at the child, and just talk to that child, play with the child and do something that you would have loved at that age, until they are happy again. Once they are then you must ask them if they trust you to look after them, this is important as it tests whether you now trust yourself, when and only when, they say yes, and you have a picture in your mind of that happy child, make that picture brighter, bolder, make the colours stronger and more vivid. Now blow that picture up in your mind so that it reaches heaven and down to the centre of the earth, let it be so big that it stretches miles and miles to each side of you, and take a massive deep breath and breathe in the feeling of happiness filling that child until it absolutely fills you.

When you can feel that love and happiness inside then, in your mind shrink that picture down until it fits into the palm of your hand and place your hand over your heart. Let that picture with its bright colours, its feelings of love and joy melt back into your heart to be kept there forever as the memory you now hold. This happy child has now melted back inside of you, no longer a sad or frightening memory but a vivid, colourful, bright, happy smiling child now an integral part of the stronger, protective adult. The one who now loves and protects yourself and knows that the pain that was once associated with that memory has gone for ever, and happiness and love have replaced that pain.
It will now be worth checking in with yourself to see if any emotion exists when you think of that memory.

Take ten or so deep breaths and   ask yourself the following questions, remembering that you want the very first word that comes to your head.

Give me an emotion:
Give me a colour:
Give me a form:
Give me a shape:
Give me a number:
That age or that many years ago?
If there is no emotion or feeling now, then you can stop here but if there is then just use the standard visualisation to destroy and overcome anything at all still left to mop up.
Do not leave anything even a 1 or a half of emotion, it must be removed completely to be a permanent release.

A working example for you to see this in operation:

This is one that I used on myself during the period of my own emotional re-tuning.

Once I had told my abusive ex that I was not prepared to keep him any longer, my first emotion was shock that I had actually done it and that I had not been harmed, I quickly left the room because I knew how easy it was for him, to make me feel guilty and he was already yelling at me that I was throwing him out on to the streets, that he had nowhere to go, and that he could not afford to pay someone rent and that I had no idea what I was doing. He was certain that I would never going to be able to manage on my own.

Although I had already agreed that he could stay for five months longer than I wanted, he was in his forties and was living with his parents when I met him and he had a girlfriend with whom he had lived before, so I knew he had two options at least, I knew that had I stayed there I would have ended up giving in and I would then never have been able to move on. I had to carry this through. I had already had some suicidal thoughts over the previous few months when I could see absolutely no other way out and I was not prepared to let him win in that way.

I went out for a walk to ensure that the conversation could not continue and started to wonder if it was my fault, and my thoughts degenerated quickly into perhaps he was right, should I give him another chance, because after all, most things seemed to be caused by my actions. By the end of my walk, however, I had cleared my mind and knew that I had to stick to my guns. Whilst I am human and not perfect by any means, I kept him, cooked for him, took all the phone calls he would not answer, took on pupils that he dumped just because he did not like them or because he couldn't be bothered to teach any more. He had no issues with himself, but he had issues with me, and I clearly had an issue with me. It needed to be sorted out for me to move on.

One evening I decided to do some therapy on myself and unearthed a belief that it was my fault, this came from when I was six. It took me a while to remember, but when I was six my brother would have been four and My Dad used to take us to the park. I finally recalled an incident when we were on a see saw, my dad was helping my brother and I was proudly doing all the work on my end myself. My mind has always had a propensity to wander (probably why my exam results weren't better!) and my brother had slid off his end but I hadn't noticed and, I had carried on, the other end of the seesaw caught my brother under the chin, I love my little brother to bits and always have and whilst my mind was undoubtedly on it usual pink fluffy cloud, I was not aware of the situation until I got shouted at, regarding how selfish I was , my brother was hurt and crying and when my Dad recounted the story to my Mum he shouted at me again and asked how I could be so horrid, so stupid and so irresponsible and I ran away to my room.

Whilst this type of situation undoubtedly happens within every family everywhere in the world, I had to take the telling off twice and was never allowed to say a word. This memory came to me and I realised that when my ex shouted at me and told me how pathetic and ridiculous and useless I was and started throwing things, I had words in my head but never had the ability, the strength or opportunity to speak them, I was literally frozen in fear and so I was getting told repeatedly, and had also long since "learned" to accept that this was in fact the case because I "knew" deep inside that it was my fault, (based on my own childhood belief) so he must in fact be right.

When I challenged this belief in my mind I asked myself was the belief true, it was not. Absolutely no one was to blame, I was six and not concentrating, my brother got hurt, my Dad was worried, and clearly panicked and felt guilty as he was responsible for us both, in a split second he clearly reacted in panic, as anyone would, needed to check that my brother was ok, so he never had time to question me, just piled us in the car and we went home.

In my adult years the fear, contained within that repressed memory, which I had buried at the age of six, was still causing me to be unable to speak up when accused, I had to do something and decided to work on the poor six-year-old me. I bought down my energy with my breathing and visualised the little girl in her room alone and crying. I picked her up and cuddled her for ages (something that the adult me needed just as much), I Took her in my visualisation to my Nan and Grandad's house where she was always made a fuss of and treated like a princess. I picked her up and comforted her again. I told her that it was not her fault, it was an accident,

I told her that I would always listen to her and help her so that she was no longer alone, and what's more I guaranteed to protect her from that day forward, and ensure that she was always heard, she would always have a voice, my voice. I also promised her that once he had gone, I would never again allow anyone into her life who did not love and respect her, or who treated her unkindly and that unless someone very gentle, kind and loving came along, it would just be me and her for the rest of our lives. Finally, at the age of 47 that little girl became important to me. She was now a very happy little girl, she trusted me because I finally put her first, I loved her and respected her and whilst it was more than forty years late, we both got healed that day. I made the picture bigger, the colours brighter and bolder, felt love and safety as I shrunk it back and placed it and the feelings behind my promises to her deep into my heart.

I went on to forgive myself for the accident, to forgive my Dad who must have been worried sick. It was shortly after this that I did my affirmations mentioned before, to change my beliefs that I was useless, pathetic and ridiculous which had been installed during the previous three years.

Chapter sixteen
Self Esteem

Self-esteem is the subjective emotional evaluation of ourselves, in other words what we deem to be our own self-worth. In our modern society we are bought up to put others first, we are taught that it is wrong to consider yourself before others, we are told that love for yourself is a negative thing and that people who love themselves are conceited and arrogant. Whilst there are occasions where an individual might consider themselves too good for others, which can never be true, generally we are conditioned by society to accept that we are not good enough on our own. Our consumer society will train you to believe that if you wear the right clothes, if you fit a certain stereotype, or if you own the right car, you can make yourself worth so much more, people will love you, people will respect you, people will want to be around you, these "things" make you a better person.

The truth is that we should always put ourselves first. Of course, moderation in all things is important, but if you do not like or love yourself, how can you honestly like or love others? If you can't be honest with yourself, how can you be honest with others? Most people spend a lifetime looking for happiness, for love, for peace, for comfort and security, but they are looking in the wrong place, they are looking outside for something or someone that will provide that which they want to feel inside. They are looking for "things" to make them feel happy, confident, attractive, etc. They are looking for experiences to enjoy, and they are looking for people who make them feel loved, valued and cared for. One thing is for absolute certain. You will never find What you are looking for until you **become** what you are looking for.

Your ability to love others is limited only by your ability to love yourself.
Your ability to find happiness is only limited by your ability to be happy.
Your ability to find peace is limited only by your ability to be at peace.

We look outside for that which we want to feel inside, yet how would you know if you have found it if you don't know what it is?

Almost every adult that I have ever met knows exactly what they are really looking for in another person, whether they are thinking about friends or a life partner. There are certain traits that are important to us and we naturally look for someone who has these traits. I have so many times spoken to friends or clients alike and they will tell me that they are looking for a person who can make them happy, a person who will be kind to them, a person who will be interested in them, a person who will make them feel loved, a person who will make them feel secure, a person with whom they can find peace, a person who makes them feel worth something.

I too spent many years wondering why, when I was looking for all of this myself, I ended up with someone who wanted to control me and then someone who wanted to shout at me, frighten me, hurt me and make me feel useless, when all I have ever wanted was to love and be loved.I trained as a therapist and was then constantly helping people to learn to be kind to themselves, to have pride in themselves, to strengthen themselves and to love themselves.

It took me a glass wall moment and taking time out of work, to finally look at me. To make me realise that I was putting out to the world that I was not important, that I was out of control, that everything is my fault. The obliging universe saw this and needed to balance it, so I was drawn to and attracting men who did not find me important, who wanted to control me and were never to blame, Job done.

I finally realised that the only person who had the ability to make me happy, was me, the only person who could make me feel loved, was me, the only person that could make me feel at peace, was me, the only person who could make me feel secure, was me and the only person who could make me feel worth something, was the person who was currently making me feel worthless, you guessed it, it was me.I worked on my irrational beliefs, I worked on forgiving myself, and forgiving others in order to remove the burden that I no longer needed to carry for them, and I worked on replacing negative thoughts about myself with positive affirmations.

I started to be nice to myself, kind and loving to myself and honest with myself. Now I can absolutely say that I am good enough, good enough by myself, (this does not mean that I don't want to be with someone else, it just means that I do not **need** anyone or anything else in order to feel complete, I am enough). I am worth loving and I deserve it, what's more someone else will need to deserve my love, because I respect and care for myself, and because I do, I know, from experience that I can love, respect, be honest, kind and gentle, generous and nurturing to someone else because I do it for myself.

Now I am showing the universe that I deserve someone with all of these qualities because they are what I feel for myself and what I have to give to someone who deserves me. I look around me now, and realise that my whole friend group has changed, many saw me changing and have just disappeared from my life. I suddenly have a group of people, around me, who are really important to me, because I am important to me, friends, to whom I can comfortably say I love you, and they do to me, and it is meant. I would never have said that to a "mate" before, it wouldn't feel right, but then it would never have felt right to think it or say it to myself.

For many years I had two very important friends, with whom I had completely lost touch when I lost touch with myself. On the day that I had the melt down, and later went on to finish the abusive relationship, I wrote letters. One to each of them, explaining how sorry I was and how rubbish I had been, both wrote back immediately. I had seen neither of them or spoken to them in over ten years and we picked up like it had been ten minutes. I am now, surrounded by the sort of people that I value and love, however, this only happened since I learned to value and love myself. As you know, there is no such thing in life as a co-incidence.

As an individual we would ideally be happy and comfortable with and confident in the person that we see in the mirror. This would therefore be us totally in tune with our authentic self, true to our soul, no pretence, no ego, just totally comfortable in who we truly are. Many people, however, suffer with self-esteem issues to a greater or lesser extent. I am sure that we have all met someone who has an inappropriately large ego, whilst this can just mean that their self-esteem is high, they have a big personality and they are very confident, conversely this can also be a mask, behind which hides a damaged soul with low self-esteem.

It makes no difference if you are a nervous school child or a hugely successful actor or pop star, with everything in the world seemingly available to you. Very often, those with low self-esteem find a way of "coping" with it, perhaps by hiding behind a persona, which they use as a mask to shield their vulnerability from the outside world, or by complete avoidance, they rarely seek help, perhaps only actually facing things when a "symptom" becomes too unbearable to live with.

Many people are not aware of the fact that they have an issue with self-esteem at all and are looking for external reasons for what they deem irrational behaviour, thoughts or feelings. On the other hand, others are very aware and either feel ashamed, embarrassed or just unaware that they can get help to overcome this debilitating condition. If you do have a low opinion of yourself, or you find that lack of confidence holds you back, or even if you find certain negative patterns playing out repeatedly in your life, then it is time to make yourself important, it is time to become the person that you are looking for. Once you no longer look externally for that which makes you happy internally then you will not only realise that you are already complete, but you will find that without effort, you suddenly attract a very different experience, different situations and different people into your life. Your reality is a mirror. So, how do you start? How do you do that?

The very first thing that you need to do is take stock. Take a good, hard look at yourself and be completely honest. Set aside some time, some time that you can completely give to yourself, for yourself. Turn the phones off, no TV, no radio and no interruptions. If you are currently thinking "there is no way I could do that, it just is not possible, practical or necessary" then believe me, you have low self-esteem, you do not value yourself enough, so why should anyone else? It really is time, time for you.

Once you have set aside this quiet time then you need your whiteboard or paper and pen, you will know, if you have read the earlier chapters if there is other work that you need to do first. If you haven't been through the finding yourself exercise, then that is the first thing, then work on any unwanted beliefs that you have, as negativity needs to be shifted for positivity to find a place. If you have done this already or, have no limiting or self-sabotaging beliefs then you are working simply on your self-esteem.

In this case your starting point is to have two columns, the first you need to put down everything about yourself, your good points, your bad points, what you like and what you don't about yourself and be honest. if you find that that you have nothing but negativity then your self-esteem is desperately low so carry out the use the eyes of another technique and do the same exercise but from a different perspective, i.e. that of someone who loves you and knows you well.

In the second column write down a list of qualities that would be very important to you in your perfect partner, someone with whom you would want to spend the rest of your life. Make it realistic, rich is not a quality, you are looking for personality, if it helps, here is mine:

Kind
Gentle
Considerate
Caring
Affectionate
Tactile
Fun
Loyal
Honest
Faithful

Next cross reference the two columns and strike off your 'desired' list any already on your 'Me now' list
You will now have a list on the desired side of qualities that are important to you but not intrinsically part of you yet. These are what you need to work on one by one. For example if honesty is important to you then you need to not only be happy that you are genuinely

honest but that you would feel comfortable to allow someone else the space to be honest with you, so they could say what they genuinely feel and you would not get defensive, or aggressive or storm out, but if you want the ability to be honest you must give someone else this space, meaning that the two of you would share an open, honest relationship.

Work through every one of these emotions, being completely true to yourself but do so one by one, if necessary use a positive affirmation to install that which you do not feel you currently have. This could take weeks or months, but no one else can do this work for you and make you feel good, you have to do the work because if you want something different, you have to do something different. Trust me, you are worth it. This is a big investment in time, however if you do this thoroughly your self-esteem will rise, you will embody all that you want in someone else, then, you are enough, you have found the person that you have been looking to attract When you get to such a place within yourself, you show the world the person that you are, your reality is a mirror and what the universe sees it will balance by giving back to you.

Chapter Seventeen.
Forgiveness

We have touched on forgiveness earlier, however, I wanted to explain the importance of forgiveness in more depth. Strangely, we as human beings often find it hard to forgive, I say strangely because the very fact that we are human, means that none of us can be perfect all of the time, and yet, we struggle to remember the same of others, and indeed, just as often, ourselves.

When we believe that we have been wronged by another, or, maybe, we, ourselves do something that we wish we hadn't, we generally have a really hard time forgiving. The problem here, is that if it is another person who has caused the issue, we often see the person and the deed as one. We can feel anger, resentment, hurt, betrayal, all sorts of feelings, but we all too often attach the feelings to the person and not the incident. Generally, if we feel strongly enough, a memory sticks in our mind. As you already know, a memory with an emotion attached to it will be filed, however, it can and, chances are it will, come back to haunt us. Maybe we will, after such an incident, act differently in a similar situation, but with a different person, and we may well not treat them as we would normally have done, simply because our subconscious mind is holding negativity from the previous experience. Often it is the emotion that will re-surface and cause us to behave in a way that we and/or others do not expect.

If the negativity has been bought about by another person, it is generally only the victim, who holds on to the memory of the event and the unpleasant emotion. The person responsible will rarely even recollect what happened, let alone hold any regret or sorrow. If they had that feeling, they would either have acted differently in the first place, or they would have apologised at the time. By holding onto this pain what you are actually doing is allowing the other person, and the memory, to hold power over you and your emotions.

It is important to understand that we actually make that choice. By accepting what was said or done to us but holding a negative feeling attached to it you may form a belief (generally not a positive one), and/or allow it to continually colour how you will deal with the person or that situation in the future. Furthermore, you will be holding onto negative thoughts, which are easily turned into a weapon with which to attack yourself, especially at times when you are already low. There is, however, the option to choose to take any lesson that might be learned from the experience and forgive that person in order that you can move on. You cannot forgive the deed, it is done, and as I mentioned earlier it can't be undone, however, when we chose to forgive, we take the sting out of its tail and file it as a benign memory. We forgive the person and accept, that right at that moment they were incapable of doing any better.

This same ability to forgive is also available to us, to ourselves, but we are very often the last person that we remember to forgive. We do things, say things, or act in a certain way and can either at the time or at some future point, regret what is said or done. We are just as able to hang on to, and hold regret, embarrassment or whatever emotion we feel, together with our recollection of what happened. In this instance what we tend to use that memory for, is to beat ourselves up time and time again. It is done, if appropriate we should apologise, and then forgive our self. Don't give your own mind, not only the power, but also the ammunition, to constantly beat you up, for what was, one single moment in time, in which we made a bad decision, a mistake, said or did something, that on reflection, we should have handled differently. In this scenario, there is almost always learning to come from the whole incident. Take the learning, forgive yourself, and move on. By doing so, you free yourself from the inner torment, caused by allowing yourself to hang on to and be controlled by guilt.

Chapter Eighteen
Habits and coping mechanisms

Sometimes a way of finding a belief can take no more than awareness. There are things that we do, often unconsciously, that are, in fact raising an awareness or, even helping us to cope with something that we don't even know is there. I once had a lady come to me wanting to give up smoking, she was in her late forties and had been smoking since she was in her twenties. I asked her why she wanted to stop, she said that she feared that now she was getting older that her health was not as she would like it to be, and she did not want to die early of any condition that she could have done something about.

Habits can become so ingrained and such a part of our day that we are unaware of how often we repeat them, and what exactly it is that we are doing. I will use smoking as an example. I asked my client how many cigarettes she smoked a day, she said that she was smoking a packet of twenty a day, this answer needed no pause or thought. I then asked her how much she was spending a day on cigarettes. This time she needed to stop for a moment, and then she said that she was spending just over seven pounds a day on her cigarettes. I went through the usual calculations with her "so you are spending basically £50 a week and she agreed, then £2548 per year, this shocked her, it always does, when people look at their habits in real terms financially. They can always think of what they could do with that money if they hadn't spent it on something to set light to.

The next part of the discussion is where things get even more real, I asked her what ingredients were in the cigarette smoke that she was inhaling. She immediately said nicotine and I added yes, and tar like they use on roads, formaldehyde which is embalming fluid, cyanide a poison and pest killer – the list is just over thirty ingredients long and none of them pleasant.

My client was paying more than £2,500 per year in order to ingest (albeit very small doses at a time) a mixture of toxic substances and she was doing this voluntarily, twenty times a day. The look of shock on someone's face, when they realise what they do without thinking, never ceases to amaze me. Of course, it isn't only smoking, but drinking to excess, drug taking, comfort eating and many other, seemingly innocent sociable and recreational activities, can form a habit. I have not yet come across any person, be they client, or friend, who has ever consciously considered their habits and really asked themselves what they are doing and, why they are doing it, prior to coming to therapy where they pay someone to help them.

A habit will be based on one of two things. Firstly, it can be what we call an empty habit, one which their body has just got used to and there was no particular trigger which started the behaviour, and in fact, people will generally not even know why they still do it. These types of habit rarely respond well to hypnotherapy or similar therapeutic methods. The reason being that the person can provide no reason for the behaviour nor any reason to stop. The body and mind have just got used to and become dependent on, the action itself or the chemicals that enter the body as a result of the action.

The other potential reason for a habit is an emotional one, this tells us that the habit was initiated as a coping mechanism for a belief and actually the person "gets something out of it" for example, a young person may have started smoking because of peer pressure, all their friends were doing it, and they felt left out, so started smoking in order to not be excluded from the social gathering at break times with all their friends. In this instance the belief that is running within the subconscious mind, regarding smoking is "I am accepted as the same as my friends (conforming behaviour) and I get fun social time by smoking" but then, the nicotine triggers the reactors in the brain and the body "needs" a cigarette and that forms the habit. So, the brain gets to "need" the substance but the subconscious believes that smoking is essential for acceptance socially and therefore, it is something 'needed' by that individual. Similarly, within families in certain cultures, alcohol forms an important part of the family get together at evening meal times, so the subconscious brain associates' alcohol as something we do as part of the family.

In this case the brain registers that drinking is what we do if we want to enjoy family time, the alcohol causes feelings of relaxation and fun being with the family and even if the habit then gets out of hand, the alcohol is associated with good times by our mind, and the person struggles to see any problem with their habit. Sometimes the person starts then to believe, that they cannot have a good time without alcohol.Most habits are carried out so subconsciously, that it is possible to not even know what you are doing at that time.

We all have habits, I am a big "list maker" I feel that if I do not write down everything that needs doing, and when, that I will forget about it and it will not be done, so I tend to have my diary, I have my weekly diary re-written on my white board, and I write a paper list of the jobs that need doing. This may seem organised; however, it took me a while to realise, that my task list often has all the jobs that need doing during that week on it, and I cannot tell you how demoralising it is when you first look at a list with twenty jobs, and the impact that your mood then has on your productivity.

During my 'dark' years when I really was low and even to a lesser extent, prior to that I used to set my own bar way too high and make my lists unachievable, I never realised what I was doing to myself, but having so much to do, and not getting it done, further backed up my belief that I was out of control and there was nothing that I could do about it. For years I was repeatedly told that I was useless, pathetic etc. it all fitted nicely with what I already believed. Awareness is the key here, so whether you have habits that you know about or not, it is worth taking one whole day and trying a little experiment. Write down, literally, every single thing that you do, even going to the loo, washing your hands, drying your hands etc. nine people out of ten will have something, usually unnecessary, that they do of which they are not even aware. It could, like my own case above, be detrimental to your mood, your time, or yourself. At the end of the day or the day after, look at your list. If there is anything that you did not realise or anything that you were unaware of ask yourself these questions:

What did you do?

What do you get from it?

Is it beneficial and improves you or your day or is it self-sabotaging?

What lies at the bottom of it?

When did it start?

Why did it start?

Why do you still do it?

Do you do it for the original reason?

What triggers doing it?

Is it when you are alone?

Is it in company?

This may do no more for you than buy you back a bit of time each day, if, for example, you maybe do something four times and it only needs doing once, or not at all, Alternatively, it may alert you to something that you do which is either backing up a belief, which you may find as a result of this exercise, or that is being used to sabotage your mood or your feelings about yourself.Now that you have had a chance to check whether there are any empty or destructive habits that you might have, it is time to see if you are employing any coping mechanisms that you may be unaware of.

If you have found a habit that you were unaware of, you need to understand if it started recently or, for a particular reason. Possibly it is something that you have always done and have no idea when or why it started. Mostly these things have no related issue and you may have found many of these if you carried out the exercise above, however, occasionally they can be a form of coping mechanism. which could be hiding a belief, a fear, some cause of anxiety, or as a way of releasing or controlling emotion. Under these circumstances, it is important to consider if this is something which is. a coping mechanism, and if so what it is that you are not dealing with that causes such a situation

As an extreme example I have mentioned before, that victims of abuse or bullying, will occasionally resort to self-harm -this can take many forms, cutting themselves, burning themselves, punching themselves or solid objects until it hurts, there are many ways. They may be self-harming in order to prove to themselves that they can control something, as when subjected to abuse, or bullying for example they have no control, or they may be punishing themselves for "allowing" something to happen to them or for what they see as their own weakness, stupidity, failings, or any other negative personality trait.

I have used an extreme example here to draw your attention to the cause and effect because there are many ways in which people "punish" themselves or release emotion such as anger, frustration, hurt, emotional or physical pain without necessarily realising it, furthermore there are actions which we carry out because our subconscious brain is trying to communicate with us and these are the times we must start to listen.

I had a client who came to me with anger issues, he would get frustrated and angry very quickly and resort to thumping walls or destroying things, for anyone watching it can be an exceptionally frightening experience, but for him venting his anger in this manner, was acceptable if he is only destroying inanimate objects. This behaviour would be triggered by something often very insignificant, He was very aware that the violence with which he reacted was often disproportionate to the trigger, however, he lost control very easily.

Alternatively, if he felt that there was something that he should have been able to do, and he had not got it right, a similar reaction took place. When questioned why he felt the need to release anger in this way, he stated it was the only way to rid himself of the feelings as they would be so very intense. Whilst extreme, this was a coping strategy, the cause was extreme emotion which he had never been able to deal with. This poor man would hold any emotion inside until his brain released adrenalin because it felt as if he were in stress and this physical response helped to ensure that the adrenalin was used and no longer held in his body.Whilst the reaction seems inappropriately dramatic for the trigger, what was in fact happening, was that a deeply repressed issue about which he had no conscious recollection, was being triggered each time he felt a loss of control.Less dramatic examples are comfort eating to excess, suddenly starting nail biting, increased or inappropriate consumption of alcohol, or using recreational drugs as self-medication for stressful situations.

There are many reasons that can initiate the start of a new habit, and I am not in any way saying that these are all coping mechanisms, but they can be. If you suddenly become aware of a habit forming or, are asked why you are doing something and you don't actually realise what you are doing, it is worth stopping for a moment looking at the action, working back to when you started it to find out what may have caused it.

Being aware of the early warning signal and looking for the cause, using the techniques covered earlier, can save you a lot of time and money if ever the symptom got out of control. You can effectively use the questioning technique to see if you can bring up feelings regarding a situation in the past, which the current action is triggering. If there seems to be no reason for it then it will generally be simply an empty mindless habit, and in this case, a little awareness will allow you to stop it pretty quickly.

Chapter Nineteen.
Your environment and your moods

There are many factors that can affect us. Feelings can be initiated by lots of things: Hormones, another person's attitude or how we are treated by other people, to name but a few. A job which we do not enjoy, or even just a "bad day at the office" (even if we generally love our job) can affect us as can illness, relationship problems (either with a partner or within your family or friendship group). Oversleeping causes us to rush around, trying to catch up then you spill coffee down your shirt, the car won't start, or you miss the bus and like a line of dominoes one thing after another goes wrong.

One thing that is often overlooked, that can have a serious impact on how you feel, is your immediate environment. Think for a moment where you spend your time. For many of us, the majority of our day is spent at work, college, school etc and therefore there is often little that you can do to change very much, however it is worth bearing in mind that dark or dingy surroundings, lack of natural light, lack of windows and fresh air, dark coloured décor or dirty surroundings, all of these things can have a subliminal effect on your mood. If once you get home, you have the same sort of surroundings, or if you are in an unhappy place, a bad relationship, you are alone, and you don't want to be, or if you are in a crowded living space with no place to escape, these things can all have the same effect.

A simple example of this is that my White board gets used for many things, and at one point I was considering some updating in the house, so I used this board, to list all the jobs that needed doing. Having had it, propped up against the wall, opposite where I sit, in my lounge, I was aware one day of reading through it and I let out a massive sigh. The 53 jobs on the board drew my attention to every bit of the house which needed work, however tiny a job was, for example, I needed a replacement bulb in the fridge, it was written down. I had been encouraging myself for weeks to focus every time that I went to relax for the evening, on a whole lot of work that the house needed. Considering nothing was urgent, I was looking at months of work and felt deflated just by sitting down to rest at the end of the day. needless to say, once I realised what I was doing to myself, I cleared the board and replaced it with what I felt happy or proud about, so it became a list of my recent achievements. Therefore, instead of something to depress me, now I could look at things that I had done recently, to make a difference to myself or others. I could look at one or two of the items on the list, smile and get on with my evening.

How and when we choose to motivate ourselves has more impact than you can imagine. Here are two examples of a potential thought process, and what the outcome will most likely be.

For illustration purposes we will imagine that our lady below, has just accepted a proposal of marriage and is thinking about the wedding:

"I need to lose weight for this wedding, I am fat and will be a fat ugly bride otherwise, and the photos will be awful, and I will be embarrassed".

The most likely outcome here, is that this lady will lose a little weight, she will be as miserable as anything, it will be a massive chore and it will go straight back on after the wedding, then she will constantly beat herself up by not being able to get back to her wedding weight. This lady has a negative attitude and that will breed a negative experience of trying, and a negative result. She is using a stick to beat herself up and this is undoubtedly coming from an un-real belief which has damaged her self-esteem.

The alternative way of motivating yourself would look more like this:

"I can't believe he proposed to me, I am so excited and so very lucky, I am going to work really hard and lose this weight because I want to walk down that aisle feeling and looking amazing and show him just what a fantastic choice he has made, and exactly what I am capable of. The Photos will be stunning, and it will be the best day of our lives."

This lady is motivating herself with a lovely day, feelings of pride and how fortunate she is. Here she is using these as a "carrot" by which to motivate herself. Her journey will be easier, more enjoyable and undoubtedly more successful plus she is way more likely to keep the weight off after her wedding.

Have a think about how you motivate yourself. I for one know that the old, broken me would most definitely have been our first example but because I am mindful of how I treat myself again these days I can honestly say that the second approach would always be mine now.

So next time you think about something that you need to do, consciously consider how you task yourself, be aware of the words that you are saying and ask yourself, would I speak like that to my best friend? If not, it is time that you started being kind to yourself, and trust me, there is no time better than right now.

Be kind to yourself

When was the last time you really, and I mean really, looked after you? I have used this analogy earlier but in the event of an aeroplane crash, unless you first secure your own oxygen mask, you are of no use to anyone else. We are bought up learning to respect others, be kind to others, be polite and courteous at all times. When have you ever heard a parent saying to a child "be nice to yourself" or "be a bit kinder to yourself".

We are taught from a very early age to look outside first, our parents would most likely have been bought up the same way and in Victorian times and prior to that, children were to be "seen and not heard" so especially in this scenario the child is taught from birth that they are not considered as equal to their parents.

Whilst it is certainly our duty, to facilitate learning in our children, and for them to grow up with social skills which will set them in good stead for life, we omit to teach children generally to love and respect themselves. Many do not suffer negatively and generally, society has a proportion of people who learn for themselves, that they need to have a strong regard for who they are.

I have covered this in quite some detail in the self-esteem chapter, but it is really important to remember, that the only person who is actually capable of making you happy is you. You need to look after you first, that is how you can learn to treat others well. I will repeat something here, that you have heard from me before, but I think that you need reminding of. Treat yourself like someone you love.

Create yourself a mission statement

Now this might sound a little crazy, however, bear with me. Life has a habit of getting in the way, we know that, and sometimes this can send you off on a tangent for days, weeks, months or even years, before you suddenly remember that you were once working towards something.

Companies use mission statements to effectively communicate to their staff, their clients and the world, what it is they stand for. This becomes, in effect, a call to action. Such a statement presents the purpose of the business to the outside world (external benefit), whilst serving as a reminder to all staff, what the company's aim, standards, purpose and aspirations are (internal benefit).

A mission statement therefore motivates staff, sells the product or service and means that everyone within the organisation is working towards the same goal. In reality we can all compare ourselves to a business. We all have a "shopfront" which is the way we present ourselves to the world, the way we dress, our mannerisms, how we look after ourselves, our attitude, how we treat others, facial expressions and body language all form part of us. We all know that a person's first impressions of us count for how they view us and will treat us in return.

We all then, also have the workforce, this is what and who we are inside. Like the business we have a face we show the world and inside is the authentic person, the soul, most people we meet on a day to day basis, at work, at school, college or university and to some degree our larger circle of friends and extended family, only ever see that facade. It is our close family and friends who actually get to see a little more of the authentic person that we are. There is only one person, however, who truly knows us, who we really are, behind that façade, and that is our self, and to be honest, as we already know, many of us never actually, take the time to discover and understand ourselves. We are the CEO or director of our own company. An ideal, and much more straightforward way of being would actually be to strip ourselves back to the authentic, real us and be confident to be ourselves, and not put on the mask which we believe, is what the person in front of us wants to see.

Take, as an example a lady we will call Jane, this lady is 34 years old, she is a wife and mother of two children, her parents are both still in her life, she has one older brother, she has a paid job working at a school, and she has a dog.

To her parents, Jane is always going to be their little girl and acts in a way that she and her parents are used to, she looks up to them, respects them, they love, help and even sometimes tell her off. Her brother went off the rails as a teenager and got into drugs and the wrong company for a while and when she was 11 he raped her, a secret they have both carried all these years to save their parents the agony of knowing the reality. So, Jane has lied to and kept this fact from Mum and Dad. Her relationship with her brother is not close but she makes it look that way for her parent's sake, so she puts on a face to hide what happened.

To her husband who has suffered with stress for many years she is the strong one holding the family together, in order to take as much pressure from him as she can, another face. To her children she is Mum, protector, she sets the rules, she cooks and cleans and does the laundry, takes them to school and helps with homework and arranges days out. To the children at school she is the teaching assistant that is fun and helps when they are afraid to ask the teacher, she is always happy and jolly and caring. To their dog she is everything, Mum, provider of food, provider of exercise and play, she takes him to the vet cleans up his toilet and pacifies him on fireworks night when he gets scared.

Jane is not her real name, but she was a client of mine and she is all of these things to all of these people and the dog, but who is she really? She is a scared little 11-year-old girl trapped in an adult body who has the strength to play all of these roles everyday but when she gets just a few minutes alone and when she sleeps, she often gets flashbacks of the rape because she kept it to herself and never dealt with it, she is tired, has low self-esteem, and suffered with anxiety and mood swings. Jane spent time with me in therapy, we released a lot of emotion and unreal beliefs, we did inner child work, hypnotherapy, Emotional Freedom therapy and positive affirmation work. She slowly managed to find, forgive and accept herself for the past and learned to forgive her brother which freed her from carrying his guilt and led to her finding more peace, and she built who she wanted to be. We used a mission statement as part of her therapy as it gave her a short description of who she really was inside and became proud of so over a period of time she was just Jane, everyone saw the same person because it was her authentically. She did not have to play different roles, she became a happier, calmer person and moved her own life on. Jane's Mission Statement was:

"I am a Beautiful, strong woman I love, respect and care for my family, friends and especially myself."

Whilst this does sound like a positive affirmation, the affirmations that we did use, were for specific healing and once she had created the appropriate and honest beliefs, she no longer needed them. Her mission statement was there to remind her of her focus, purpose and responsibility especially to find time for herself, for the rest of her life, because she now knows, absolutely, that she deserves it and she feels worth it. This reminds her to keep a balance for herself as well as others, because, she is being kind to herself, she is therefore strong and happy, which allows her to be a better daughter, wife, sister, mother and teaching assistant because she loves and respects herself. Everyone, including Jane, herself, now all see the same strong and authentic person who looks after herself as much as others in her life. Not only does this make

Jane's life easier but she is setting a fantastic example to her children.

So, a mission statement lets you look every day at a short positive and uplifting statement and describes you, your purpose and your values. If you live and work by these, all the faces that you may need to show the world disappear in favour of a single authentic person that everyone, including yourself, gets to know and respect. Your mission statement needs to be short, meaningful and concise. The one I use for myself is:

I am a strong and loving person, I work completely from my heart and soul to empower as many people as possible, to bring positive change to their lives.

When deciding what to use in your mission statement find the most important thing to you, for me it is the fact that I work from my heart and soul. Next, what it is that you wish to strive for and for me this is that I desperately want to empower others to make positive personal change. I know, absolutely, that I have the strength, love and ability to achieve this because I finally became kind and loving to myself. If you are able to add a colourful uplifting image and print and frame it, do so, you will then be constantly drawn to look at it, reminding you of your purpose and value. Even just hand writing it and sticking it on your bathroom mirror or your mantlepiece will do the trick.

Chapter Twenty.
Working examples.

In this chapter I am giving you examples of clients with whom I have worked, no identifying information is included. All symptoms and therapy are absolutely accurate, some basic information such as occupation etc. have been changed for their privacy.

I hope that these will show you how all that we have covered so far works in a real environment with real people.

The whole process in a therapy setting.

A gentleman came to me who was looking to, in his own words, "just get back on track really". This gentleman had one of the biggest hearts I have ever known but he had a feeling about him which I picked up on. He had some good friends and he had family, both parents and his two sisters were close by and yet, the whole feeling from him was that he felt lonely and isolated. He told me that he had a very fortunate life, he was not, by any means rich but comfortable, he had everything that he needed and wanted materially, but he had come to me for assistance with weight loss.

The gentleman was nicely spoken and clearly an educated man. He was six stones over weight and had been since his early twenties. At the time of his first visit to me he had just turned thirty-nine years of age and said that he wanted to get himself back in check before he entered his forties. He was well aware of the fact that he was not giving himself a good chance, health wise, going forward.

Initially we started off talking about his family and upbringing, his father was in the Army and they had moved around the world quite a bit in his younger years. Mum was the anchor of the family and had bought the children up, she had been Mum, Dad (in Dad's absence), life coach and his rock. He said that he had grown up with a very strong respect and admiration for his father. We started to talk about how his family felt about his weight. His parents were very worried about his future health, one of his sisters has a similar battle with her weight, and the other had never had an issue, had always been sporty and a "health freak" as he called her. He had no idea when he had started to feel out of control with his size nor did he have any conscious idea about any emotional trigger incidents that there may have been in his life.

I asked him to consider how he felt his parents might cope if he did nothing, and due to his weight and future health, he happened to pre-decease them. He thought for a moment and said that he had not really thought about that but that his parents were "both strong and that they would cope admirably". I then asked him how he would feel if his health deteriorated and in years to come he was unable to be there to look after his parents if they became ill. This worried him considerably more than the previous question, he got quite emotional and said that his sisters would cope. I then went on to ask him how he would feel if he and his parents needed care simultaneously due to his parents age and his health. This troubled him, but he said that between them they would fund additional care if necessary for his parents.

By this point I could see where this was going, so I asked him how he would cope if his parents died tomorrow. As I had expected, this was where he absolutely and completely fell apart emotionally. This poor gentleman felt nothing for himself at all but held his sisters and his parents in such high regard and had so much love for them that the thought of dying himself meant nothing, but the thought of his parents being taken from him (as would be the natural pattern of life) absolutely crucified him.

We moved on to what he ate and what exercise he got. He worked in a clerical setting, a very typical nine to five job, but said that there was often call for him to stay late, work a Saturday and/or take work home at the weekend. He advised me that as he was on his own, there was very little point in bothering much with cooking and that he generally bought ready meals or had food delivered. I asked about his health and he said that he had never had any real problems, he got out of breath easily, did not do any form of specific exercise but he walked a little on a Sunday if the weather was good. He had not visited the doctor in years.

My first piece of advice to him, was that although we were starting therapy, I suggested that he make an appointment with his GP to just have an "M.O.T" with the intention that he needed to make some significant changes to his diet and exercise. He looked at me somewhat quizzically, I am sure he must have realised that therapy alone would not shift the weight but for that initial second he seemed surprised. It suddenly dawned on him that he, was going to have to do the lion's share of the work. Immediately, his demeanour became a little more serious. He agreed to make the appointment prior to our next meeting.

We went on to start work, I did an initial relaxation session, this serves a dual purpose, it lets my client have a "taster" session of what hypnotherapy is, so that they can see if it is something that they enjoy and are comfortable with, and I can see how effective this therapy will be for them. The relaxation is simply that, I invite my client to sit back and relax in a position that suits them, I ask them to slow their breathing and be very conscious of it and explain that they can close their eyes straight away or whenever they feel ready.

On that first session we work through a progressive muscle relaxation, that is to say that they systematically take their conscious mind to various parts of the body and relax the area that they are working on. Once they are completely relaxed I give them a couple of moments before we come back to the present, but this session shows me and also the client, if this is one technique we should use for their tailored therapy. The next step is to ask some of my quickfire questions just to establish if there are any underlying beliefs that show themselves once the client is relaxed and in touch with their authentic self.

At this point we came up with an incident at 6 years old whilst his Dad was away working and someone broke into the house early one morning, he heard his Mum scream and a man's voice, terrified he hid in the corner of his room between the wardrobe and the side wall, His Mum was crying and he froze, unable to move, and he recalled being so frightened that he wet himself. It was only a few moments before his mum came up stairs to check on the children, she had disturbed an intruder, who had run away immediately that she screamed, however as far as this little boy was concerned, his Mother was being attacked. I asked him what belief that little boy formed about himself of the world right then and he said "We are not safe and it's my fault" I asked if there were any further thoughts or feelings that he had, surrounding that night, and he said that he had always felt guilty. When I asked why, at six, he would feel guilty, he told me that every time his father went away, he would pat my client on the head, and say, you are the man of the house, look after our girls.

My client was carrying the fear of the trauma (from the child's perspective) and he was carrying the guilt for not protecting his family, as his father had "instructed" him to do. Not that in any way any other person, including his father had ever said anything of the sort to him. This poor man had held this belief, unconsciously for 33 years but not dealt with it. He was aware of the guilt and he did get flashbacks which, whilst still occurring, were getting less and less in number over the years. Because he had not addressed the issue and was still holding it, his body had wrapped him in many layers of "protection" and the guilt had, over the years, eroded his self-esteem and it was clear that he did not like himself, let alone love himself. He had held on to the belief that he should have protected his mother and sisters, albeit an irrational thought that a six-year-old boy could, in any way, have challenged a grown intruder, he formed resultant beliefs regarding himself that he was not good enough, he was weak, he was a coward, he was irresponsible and was not a man.

He had no comprehension whatsoever, that this childhood incident was in anyway linked to his current issues as all of them had appeared much later in life, they included low self-esteem, his weight together with his lack of ability to move further in his career and his life. He was completely aware of having the ability to progress, but just could not "bring himself to try". He stated clearly that he believed that his weight was affecting his confidence. I explained that his weight was a symptom as much as the low self-esteem. We worked for several months. We started off with taking the emotion out of the traumatic event and destroying the beliefs that he had formed, that in itself, allowed his confidence to start growing, because we had removed the foundation for some of his self-deprecating thoughts. We then worked on his self-esteem. Next, we worked on the weight using positive affirmations, hypnotherapy and conscious habit changing. He gradually introduced and made exercise an important part of his life. Slowly, changes to his eating habits were making a difference and whilst he still had a way to go, when he felt capable of continuing on his own, he had lost four stones whilst he was working with me and was enjoying the process of rebuilding himself.

Example 1. Finding the belief.
Whilst working as a driving Instructor I had a client who came to me because I was a female Instructor. She was petrified of driving. She was nearing her 50th Birthday and had tried on many occasions to learn to drive and this was going to be her last attempt. She was

very capable of driving the car, but her nerves reduced her to tears within minutes of getting in on the driver's side of the car even whilst we were parked in a safe, off road area. She told me that she had tried to learn to drive with about twelve other instructors over the years previously but never managed to get to test because of her nerves She now she felt pressured to obtain her licence as her husband had become quite ill and could no longer drive so it was a necessity if they were to stay mobile. We set to work building her confidence very slowly and then we went out on the road, she did well for about twenty metres until we encountered another car at which time she screamed and took both hands off the wheel. At this point we both decided that maybe we ought to work on her before we worked on the driving! She then came to me as a therapy client. When we sat down and went through the questions these were the answers that she gave:

Colour **red**
Number **seven**
Seven years old
Shape **triangle**

When I asked her what belief, she formed right at that moment she said "I'm not safe"
I asked her what, at the age of seven was a unit of three (normally family or friends, situations etc) she said it would have been her and her parents. My next question was; did anything happen at that age to make her feel unsafe. She seemed quite surprised but recalled that there had been a car accident, she described an accident on a local country road when she was about that age, her Dad had lost control of the car on a bend in the

road, the car had spun and left the road and although it was not at dramatic speed because of the road, the car was quite damaged and got written off as it hit a tree. Whilst there were no serious injuries and no other vehicles were involved she had been reading and only paid attention when the car started to slide. I asked her to visualise that time and, to reconnect with the emotion as she felt the car slide and hit the tree. I asked her to tell me what she felt about herself or the world at that time and she said, "We are going to get hurt".

She said that she knew that her Mum had always been a nervous passenger but that she had pretty much forgotten about the accident years ago. She had, until that point, assumed that as her Mum was nervous, she had picked her own driving anxiety up, as a result. Through all the years that this lady had tried to learn to drive, she had always told potential instructors that she was nervous, had a couple of lessons and discontinued so there had been no opportunity for her to build her confidence. No one had ever asked her why she was nervous and because she herself, knew that her Mum got petrified in the car, she had assumed that was the cause. She had no idea that she was holding the trauma of this previous accident because the detail had clearly been repressed.

We worked that day on using the visualisation technique she started as seeing the red triangle (a warning road sign close to the accident) as like a wall which was many times the size of her, she slowly felt that it got smaller and smaller and she was ultimately able to step over and walk away from it, We did quite a lot of therapy work in one session and although rebuilding her confidence in the car took a while to come, it was easier for her every time. She passed her driving test first time and is driving around now, with her grandchildren, in her own car and I have passed her out on the roads many times.

Example 2. Greif

A lady came to me for assistance, some years ago, because her work occasionally involved her talking to people who had lost a friend or family member for whom they had been caring. Her task was to help them build their confidence and help and support them whilst they moved their own lives on following their loss. She had always loved her job with a passion but found it difficult to keep her own emotions under control whilst she was working in this way. She had assumed she was just very empathic, however, she was finding it harder and harder and had begun crying regularly, whilst working and she had absolutely no idea why, because she had never been in their situation, caring for a loved one, and therefore, her lack of control felt inappropriate to her and irrational.

The lady could be a bit anxious naturally, so we started off with some relaxation work in hypnotherapy which calmed her nicely, and she was sufficiently relaxed to start work. I asked her lots of the quick fire easy personal questions in order to get her conscious mind "out of the way". She stormed through these and so I threw in the questions to which I wanted answers. These were her responses:

Give me an emotion: **hurt, pain**
Give me a colour: **blue**

What shade of blue: **very dark blue**
Give me a shape: circle
Give me a number: **17**
17 years ago, or age 17? - **17 years ago**

This immediately told me that 17 years ago something had made her sad and the very dark blue said healing was desperately needed. What stood out the most was the emphasis that she placed on the "very dark blue". The lady's tone, body language and diction held some real bitterness. It was clear that it wasn't only the sad event, but also, something connecting to it, meant she still had not come to terms with, or accepted whatever trigger lay within the foundation of her feelings. Furthermore, she had not dealt with the situation but had supressed something which now took control of her whilst she was working. I asked her what had happened 17 years ago, and she seemed surprised that she had bought up the time that her Father had died. She was already quite tearful, however, I needed to find out why this was ongoing (the circle – means continuous or in a loop).

I apologised that she was finding it hard, but I asked her to tell me about his passing. She said that she had spoken to him by telephone in the morning as she, herself was about to leave for an extended holiday with friends, and he was on holiday skiing. He was a fit healthy man and took regular holidays, however, she found out, upon her return one month later, from her Step Mother, that he had died of a heart attack whilst they were away but he had been cremated already , she was not close to her Step mother, and never found out why it was all dealt with so quickly, nor did she know why she was never contacted at the time It was clear that she held resentment, anger, and pain, as well as the fact that she had never been able to say goodbye to her Dad. The circle showed that she had never dealt with her grief, it continued, the healing required was vast as it was for grief, together with the other negative emotions that she was holding on to.

This lady was stuck in what we call the grief curve. When we lose someone that we love we go through a process and it can take two to seven plus years to work through it. It starts with shock and avoidance and naturally takes a person through a range of emotions which are necessary and ends up with acceptance and the ability to start to move on with our own life.

My lady did not know about the grieving process in any technical depth and honestly thought that she had dealt with her father's passing years ago. She was, however, actually stuck early in the process of grief as she had no evidence, just like a person who loses someone, say in the forces, and may be killed in action. There was, in basic terms, no body for her to see, no burial or cremation for her to attend and no opportunity to say goodbye. Her Dad had just been wiped out of her life, she could not move past the stage at which she was stuck because there was no proof. Her healing never happened, so she was sad, but the bitterness and resentment came because she was excluded and not able to say goodbye.

Clearly, when she was working with someone after they had lost a relative or friend, she was resonating with their pain and her subconscious mind was finding the pain in her. As she had never properly grieved, she had not moved on herself, she had no idea what was going on inside her and the fact that she had never faced her own feelings. I asked her what decision she made about herself or the world at that time that she was told, and she said, "I should have been with him" and I was excluded"

This lady was carrying guilt very strongly for not being there and also, resentment for the control that her Step Mum had over her. She had been excluded and so felt isolation from her family. She was clearly very emotional. I used the visualisation technique with her, I asked her to close her eyes and asked her to give me a form for this dark blue circle, that she had, and she said it was like a thick mist. I asked about her guilt and to scale it from 1 to 10, with one being barely noticing the feeling and ten being completely over whelmed. She gave me ten.

Whilst she had her eyes closed I asked her if she could have done anything from where she was at the time and naturally she said no, I asked her if she thought she could have done anything even if she could have gone to see him, she again said no. She could now "see through" the mist, I asked where that guilt was, and she said 7. I asked her to visualise her Dad as he was when she had last seen him, she could. She described him to me, I asked her if she thought her Dad would have felt that she had let him down, she said no, it was just impossible to have got to him whilst he was alive, from where she had been, again I asked her where her guilt was, now it was a 3. At this point I asked her why the guilt was there, she could not think of a single reason for feeling guilty and I asked her to check in again with the guilt that she now felt, and she said "oh God, it's gone completely.

The next thing I did was ask her to close her eyes again, and whether she was able to visualise standing next to her Dad and she smiled after a moment or two and acknowledged that she had that picture in her mind, I asked her to take his hand, her smile broadened and then I asked her if they would both take a step towards the blue mist and then if she would describe it for me now. She said it was pale blue and she could see through it and it was only a few steps away. I got her to take one step at a time towards it with her Dad and then asked her to hold his hand a little tighter and take the step which took them through this mist. I asked her to walk on several steps and then turn around and describe it and she said it has just floated away, it wasn't there any longer. I asked her to turn towards her Dad and asked her to describe him to me again, she described the most beautiful smile, his eyes, how it felt to hold both his hands and her face had visibly changed, she had stopped crying when we started the visualisation and was beaming now. I asked her to make the colours in that picture brighter and bolder and to make that picture reach the sky and the centre of the earth, she acknowledged that it was absolutely huge, bright and shining colours, then I asked her to shrink the picture down to fit in the palm of her hand, then place her hand over her heart and to allow that picture to melt into her heart and to keep it there, safe, for the rest of her life.as her last memory of her beloved dad.

At our next session we worked on her belief of exclusion and started to rebuild her self-esteem, finally I wrote her a positive affirmation and explained to her how to use it. She was now tasked with replacing the unreal beliefs that we had shifted, and she could carry on working through the process of grief with a picture surrounded by real, unconditional love for her dad deep in her heart. Furthermore, she had bought Dad back and said goodbye to him herself.

She was no longer carrying the millstone which was the guilt which had never been hers in the first place. She got stronger really quite quickly. Now that she has dealt with her own grief and the feelings that she held around it, she has no issue in working with bereaved relatives when she needs to and has, in fact, helped a couple of people who are struggling to say goodbye, by using the visualisation technique with them herself, in a gentle way. Now that she has healed and taken control back from her emotions, she pays her healing forward when she can. This in itself is one of the most beautiful ways that demonstrates how healing often does not stop with the person who initially needed it
So very often healing creates a chain reaction and goes much further than it was ever intended to. Something here, perhaps to bear in mind. You may be reading this book because you, yourself are looking for healing, or to take control, or move your life forwards. please always be aware, that if a person crosses your path with their own issues, just a few words from another, who has experience of difficulty themselves, could trigger that other soul's entire healing process. As you now know, nothing in life is a coincidence, you could, one

day become an earth angel for someone who really needs you.

Example 3.
A lady came to me for hypnotherapy who was suffering with low self-esteem, when she first came to me she had said that she felt a fraud because she and her husband had no children, they both worked full time and they had a lovely standard of living. She was of the opinion that she had no right to need therapy because they had such a lovely life, she was close to all her family and always had been. The lady had started to get anxious about going out, She believed that this had stemmed from an incident during a childhood family holiday, when she had a very bad upset stomach one day and became very ill, she couldn't control her bowels and had to keep stopping at toilets .She had always hated using public toilets any way, and was very embarrassed even if anyone around her was talking about going to the toilet or anything similar. All of these feelings were getting worse for her to the point that she was having panic attacks.

What had started as a worry about having a day out maybe with her family was now starting to affect her work, she got anxious about her ability there, she had never felt that she fitted in with the crowd anyway, and had only ever gone in, done her job, would go out for lunch so she did not have to talk to anyone and almost raced out at five when she finished. By the time she came to me, even the thought of work, or going out for a day was triggering her anxiety. It was giving her nightmares, she was waking several times a night and was emotional for no apparent reason. Just speaking to her it was clear that she had a variety of issues and whilst there was a need to investigate, the very first thing that I did was to refer her to see her GP. She was, very clearly, suffering with clinical depression and that had to be addressed first.

After a handful of weeks, she returned, the initial anti-depressants that she had been given were not suitable, so these had been changed and the depression was getting a little more under control and she felt strong enough to face working on her self-esteem. Initially we did some relaxation work and once she was able to manage her emotion and relax herself a little, we started working very gently. She began to get more and more comfortable with the hypnotherapy and so one day I felt that she was in a strong enough place to look at the cause of her current emotional state. We had spoken at length about it, but she could recall nothing in her past which would have led to these feelings. We did our normal initial relaxation and then I started with the questioning technique. Here is what we came up with:

Emotion: **fear**
Number: **3**
Age or years go: **Age 3**
Colour: **green**

I asked her what had happened outside at age 3 that frightened her, initially she had no idea but did finally ask her mum who recalled that that when she was very small she had been playing in her grandparents' garden and her Mum was chatting with her Grandad indoors she had got to the shed and managed to find some bottles of drink and had drunk some of it.

Her Nan had seen her enter the shed and came outside immediately. Suddenly, Nan pulled the bottle from her whilst her Mum ran over, stuck her fingers down the little girl's throat and shook her, forcing her to be sick. Both grown-ups were shouting, and Mum was also crying. She did not remember too much else apart from the fact that she was told some years later the empty lemonade bottle had been filled with weed killer. I asked her what decision about her or the world did she form that day and she said that all she can remember was her Grandad saying that she was stupid and that she cannot be trusted and that she was very naughty.

Of course, as an adult she understood that her family were scared and felt guilty. She did however comment that she had grown up very much feeling that people judged her and saw her as stupid and untrustworthy but had never related her current feelings to a forgotten childhood memory. To accentuate it even more, she got immediately embarrassed that she had never tied the two things together.

I reminded her that she couldn't remember the incident until we tied down the age, feeling and that it was outside.
So, we had our foundation, we had a period in her life, an event, a belief and an emotion. We were able to re-imprint the memory with some inner child work, remove the emotion from the event, we used visualisation to bring down the green box which she saw in front of her to something that she could squash and walk over. We worked on some counselling and re-framing the situation over a few weeks as this fear of

being stupid, untrustworthy and naughty had been buried so deep and was at the base of her current issues. Ultimately, she saw the situation as an adult and I asked her what she would have done had it been her niece, she agreed that in a similar situation, then panic would be her only emotion at the time as well. All that left us to do was to work through forgiving herself, and her family for the event and herself for allowing these feelings to take control of her.

Example 4.

One lady came to me because at 58, she was desperate to make some changes. This lady is five foot six, she had a sedentary job working in London. She had insulin managed type 2 diabetes since her thirties, she is married with five grown up children and eight grandchildren. She is the absolute centre of her family. She came to me at three stones over weight and with her diabetes worsening.

Her problem was that her lifestyle, being very busy, and having long train journeys twice a day, meant that for years she had lived on a fast food, take away, high sugar, high fat diet. During her working day she had few breaks, so it was off to the local burger place every lunchtime and to keep her energy up during the day chocolate bars, chocolate biscuits, sweets, crisps......then the weight went up steadily and it got out of control, she tended to hold her weight in her stomach area and yet when she came to me she said that she needed help to lose the weight, but she did not mind her tummy because that was due to having 5 children and it's just what happens to your body.

Because she was due to go on holiday in three months she was desperate to lose the weight quickly. We had quite a long consultation and I said to her that I felt that the weight was a symptom and not the problem in itself. She agreed that she was more than prepared to work with me long term if necessary but desperately wanted to work on the weight for her holiday and would then commit to therapy after that in order to find any underlying cause. This is not how I would ideally want to have proceeded, however she was so desperate that I agreed to help her, in the hope that she would keep her word and return to me after her holiday so that we could find and work on a long-term solution.

I wrote her a very tough hypnotherapy script and felt quite cruel delivering it but even though she went into a lovely hypnotic state and was very open to suggestion she cried quite forcibly when I got to the tough part of the script. When she came round she told me that she had no idea of any of the words after the early stages, but she was aware of being very upset and did not know why and I did not enlighten her! My lady lost a stone and a half before she went on holiday after only one session and was thrilled. Upon her return she made an appointment with me for one month's time. By the time that she came back nine pounds had gone back on and she was really beating herself up. It was at that moment that I very clearly saw exactly how little she valued herself and where we would find the origin of her habit.

She had made it very apparent that she was attacking herself mentally and then consoling herself with food. With such a low opinion of herself she was "self-medicating "with the very cause of her existing weight. I immediately got a picture in my head of my Dad when my brother and I were very young because he loved to play dominoes, well rather he loved to line them up and see how far he could go and then tip the first one over and watch our faces. my brother was a real giggler in those days and this "trick" of Dad's was all it often took to create ten minutes of hysteria. So, my lady was clearly holding a belief or an emotionally based habit which caused her to attack herself, and then reach for what would make her feel better. (however, her choice of self-medication only exacerbated the issue that she was trying to escape from in the first place). (let's call it the domino effect for now).

When we started working we also found out why it was that she was happy to have a very distended tummy. She dearly loved her children and she said that there were only five times in her life when she felt good about herself. That was when she was pregnant, she honestly believed that the only good she had ever done in her life was to bring her beautiful children into the world. When she was pregnant she could eat what she wanted, everyone loved her and was excited for her, her family all made a fuss of her and her husband paid her so much more attention. This lady at the time, worked in London, was a high earner and the major breadwinner for her family, raised a big family and yet had, the lowest opinion of herself that I have ever come across.

She had been fortunate enough to marry her best friend and soul mate, however, her self-critical side had come out more and more in their early years of married life, which had driven a wedge in between them so as she beat herself up more and more, and effectively she was saying to the world and especially to her husband "I am worth nothing, I dislike myself, it's my fault and I hate being me. This was subconsciously picked up by her husband over time as his affection was not returned. My client did not think that she deserved it and so acted in a way as to brush it off, so it reduced and reduced until it stopped. When she got pregnant and was concentrating on the baby inside her she started to enjoy her body and eased off and so he got more affectionate again and this carried on until the baby came and my lady no longer felt useful other than to look after the children, then the cracks appeared and slowly the divide widened again and so this cycle formed and was perpetuated.

When the lady came to me she described their relationship as brother and sister or friends but there was little affection, no intimacy and this had been how it was for more than twenty-five years. When she went on this recent holiday, however she was actually feeling very proud of herself, and rightly so. This meant that she went away happy and something that she had not felt for many years, she was relaxed. They "had the loveliest time since their Honeymoon" was the phrase she said to me, her face, body language and smile which reached so wide it appeared to originate from one eye and end at the other said it all….no more detail was necessary (if you get my drift).

This did however put her in the right place mentally for us to start work, and to find the origin of this self-destructive tendency that she had developed throughout her life. We worked hard on the first session, but it did not take long to find the oldest belief and that was one which she had formed at primary school. Her parents were devoted to her and her brother but were not well off. She was picked on at school and she specifically recalled a memory of being bullied at first school.

She ran home. The belief that she formed at the time was "I am different to everyone else and not good enough" further bullying at junior school because she was "chunkier" than her peers consolidated this, and she remembers taking money from her Mum's purse in order to buy sweets and cigarettes on the way to school. This was the start of the comfort eating and this only served to exacerbate the problem for her. She started playing up and missing school over the years which caused her to get in trouble and therefore her education suffered which served to consolidate her belief about herself.

The second belief that we found was "it's my fault" because she was getting into trouble at school, and she would not explain why she was behaving so badly, her parents enlisted the help of her Uncle who was a policeman. He came over to tea one evening to see her and started to ask her why she was behaving in the way she was. She could not answer out of embarrassment, and he went on to tell her how they "deal" with naughty and nasty young people in court.

Her parents were hoping a short sharp shock might just bring her in line, but she felt that her parents were getting into trouble because of her and so, unfortunately something, that they clearly did out of love, backfired in a way and gave the, then, adolescent cause to beat herself up even more.

It took us eight sessions to work on these, we worked with some different techniques due to the length of time that she had been controlled by her beliefs, after a few months we did a consolidation session to top up her confidence. There is a lovely ending to this lady's battle, she had been doing well since we finished, and I bumped into her some years later and she had lost her excess weight completely, after we had worked on the beliefs, and she had maintained her goal weight for over five years at that point. her required insulin levels had dropped substantially, and she was very much healthier and happier.

Example 5 (a belief, hiding a belief)
Colour – **Black**
Shape – **circle**
Form – **like a hole**
Number **13**
Age 13
Emotion – Feeling hopeless

I had a gentleman come to me for help, who was having problems holding down a job and had tried seven in the previous eighteen months. During the questioning, he saw a big black hole on the floor in front of him which was so large that there was no way round it.

His number was 13 and we established that this was the age at which he was diagnosed as dyslexic and his belief, when questioned was "there is no point".

Everything that I tried would not reduce the size of the hole so mid-sentence I asked him really quickly for another number, this caught him off guard, and it was an immediate response 5.

 He had lost his Mum who was his world when he was five and he had one horrid picture in his head of the empty grave and her coffin being lowered in to it. Here, was our big black hole. Clearly we had now found the right hole, so I asked him to close his eyes and picture his mum and he could so I asked him to visualise himself, as a five year old, holding his mum's hand and standing in front of the grave, this was emotional but he could, now the black hole was only the size of the grave, so I asked him to see himself, still holding his Mums hand and the two of them walking round the grave until it was behind them.

 He did so, now, I asked what was on the floor in front of them, he answered "just grass" I asked him then to imagine himself now, as a man standing holding his Mum's hand and turning to her. I asked him to describe his mum, as he saw her in his mind, and he said, "just my beautiful Mum, calm and happy". So, I got him to take his picture of her like that and make the colours brighter and stronger and make the picture so big it went up to the sky and down to the earth, then shrink it back until that bright happy picture fit into the palm of his hand. He did so, then I got him to put his hand over his heart which he did and put his happy mum in there, where she belonged and told him he can talk to her all the time.

By this point, He was smiling, so I asked him to just visualise turning around and looking back to where the hole was but all he could see was grass with daisies all over it – that means he was seeing a new start as daisies come in the spring. This gentleman was blaming the fact that he was dyslexic for all his troubles and believed, that there was no point because he was dyslexic and would always struggle with what his peers could do.

The truth was, that he was stuck in the grief curve at the age of 5 by the emotion that he felt at his Mum's graveside and he had never actually moved on because the 5 year old boy could not see how life could carry on without Mum As a man, he was able to see where he was stuck, rationalise why that picture was so haunting and he had finally been able to move on from his Mum's grave. I recommended that he seek grief counselling to ensure that he could start to move forward with his own life.

Example 6. Helping the inner child move on.

I once had a lady who was having self-esteem issues in her thirties. She had come to me as she had never had a nice relationship even though she got plenty of offers of dates she could not bring herself to go. We went through the questions and she gave me:

Number 8
Shape Triangle
Colour -red, pillar box red
Emotion – fear
Belief: I am going to get hurt and I will be in trouble

She was walking to school one day at about that age and a dog was off lead and bit her, she screamed and ran back home but knew her Dad was in and he had worked the night and would be asleep, he could be an angry man, so she knew she must not wake him, however, she had no key, so she hid behind the dustbins. A postman had found her there and had rung the door bell and woken her dad up who shouted at her and dragged her back to school. The triangle was her, her dad and the postman hence the pillar box red which she did not even tie up until we had located her age so, she had held the fright and pain of being bitten, and then the fear of her dad's reaction. She was also holding emotionally on to the feeling of having to hide, fear of being found, and the trouble that she would be in for not getting to school. The fear of waking her Dad was the worst of all for her.

All these emotions were causing her, as an adult, to be nervous, shy and afraid of what could happen in a situation she knew nothing about, and especially where men were concerned. Therefore, as a thirty-four-year-old lady her belief system said if she did anything that involved a man she would get hurt and she would get into trouble.

She could visualise a massive red triangle, but it was much bigger than her (not surprising as she was an eight-year-old child when it happened, and small children have to look up at most things). I asked her to see her younger child self, hiding behind the bins and she could, next I got her to see herself as an adult holding hands with the child, then I asked how the triangle looked. It had shrunk a bit, so I asked her to take five steps towards the triangle hand in hand with the little girl and she did. Then I asked her to see a door in the triangle and to open it, so they could both go through. She did that and I asked her as the adult to turn around and to lock the door with a key she would find in her right-hand pocket and she did then I asked them to walk away from the triangle ten paces, which she did, three times until I asked them both to turn around and look at the triangle neither of them could see it.

So again, what we did here was to move through the picture as the frightened child, being protected by her as an adult, go through the shape (the event) close and lock the door (on the memory which locked her angry dad and the dog on the other side) then walk 30 paces away and she could no longer see the event let alone any detail.

Example 7. Change the experience to break a habit

One of my young driving pupils could drive the wheels off of my car, she could drive for two hours, in new areas that she did not know, deal with all types of traffic. If you had got in the car with her at the point that I had her, ready for test you would not have believed that she was only 18 and would have expected that she had been driving on her own for years, yet she could not pass the practical test. The only single time that she would make a mistake would be on test, and it would be a whopper.

Every time that I picked her up on test day she was emotional and in pieces. We had several discussions about what she was thinking and what she was feeling, and she could not put her finger on it. One day I drove her home after a test and pulled over and stopped the car and she was crying about the test she had just failed, and I asked her what was going through her mind, and she said I just don't think that I can do it. (I knew differently) but she could not tell me why. I sneakily started asking her general questions about her childhood then, because she was so emotional I switched straight into the quick-fire questions, Luckily, she had not realised so did not think about her answers and I found her belief within seconds. Here is what she gave me:

Colour: **Red** – (what sort of red?) – dark red she literally spat the words out (lots of anger here then!)
Form – **Solid** – (how solid?) – **A brick wall**
How tall is this brick wall? – **I can't even see the top of it**
Shape: **Square**
Number:**11**
Age 11or 11 years go?
Age 11

When I asked her, what made her angry at 11 she cried, she had done "really badly" at her 11+and not got into the school that her parents had wanted, her sister who was two years older had got into the best school in the area. I asked her what was the worst part of that? was it her sister, the school? She said no. In a very young voice she hung her head and said I let my Daddy down.

She was the youngest and an absolute daddy's girl which I did not realise at the time. When I took her home, her parents were waiting for her at the door, she got out of the car and shook her head to them and her Dad shouted so that even in the car I could hear "you should give up, you're never going to do it and stormed off. Well, that was a like red rag to a bull to me and I called her back into the car. I asked her if she would consider some therapy to help her relax with tests and she said yes. Because I was so angry with her Dad I gave her ten session dates and I told her some would be therapy, and some would be mock tests to see how she was doing and she agreed. I told her I was trying something different and would not charge her, but she had to bring her licence as she would not know which were to be therapy and which were mocks.

On her first Session we did therapy I asked her to close her eyes and take some deep breaths to relax herself and I asked her to get that brick wall in her head. I asked her where her anger was on a scale of 0 meaning nothing and 10 meaning raging anger, she gave me a 9. So, I asked her about what she was good at and she gave me several things, mostly practical things such as cooking, writing poetry, making models, making clothes pottery etc, I got her to agree that she was very practical and asked her how good her sister was at those things, she laughed and said she will try for two and a half minutes and then say it's stupid and give up. I asked her how her results were in her GCSEs. She said well I passed them but only just, my sister got much better grades, So I asked her if they both passed though, and she said yes. I asked her where that anger was, and she said 6.

As her Mum travelled for work I asked her what the girls had to do when mum was away. She told me that She cooked and cleaned but her sister did very little as she was lazy and more into boys. I reiterated "so you cook and keep the house for you all when Mum is away?" She agreed, and I said what would happen if you were ill? she said they would get a take away. I got her to agree that she was the one who looked after Dad and her sister and I asked her how big that wall was, she said waist height. I asked her if she could get over it yet, she said maybe. I quickly asked her what was the last thing that her sister did to disappoint her dad, she smiled and said that she had misjudged the wall coming home last week and damaged her car and he had really shouted at her.

All of a sudden, her wall was nothing more than a line of bricks. I asked her to see herself, in her mind's eye, walk over it, and she did, I asked her, to stay in that picture and to look back and could she see it and she said just about. I asked her to tell me about the last time her dad was proud of her. She told me that she had one of her poems published a couple of months ago I asked her to see her dad, standing 10 paces in front of her and see his face as it was the day she had shown him the magazine. I asked her to walk up to him for those 10 paces and see herself showing him a driving test pass certificate in place of the published poem, then I asked her to describe his face and what she felt right at that moment.

She told me that he had the biggest grin and she was proud and crazy excited. I then I asked her to look back at what was left of the wall, she couldn't see it, she said it was gone. I gave her appositive affirmation and made her promise to use it many times a day over the rest of the time that we had in the diary and she committed to it.

On our second session we went straight out and did a mock test. She passed. So, we did a little re-run of her brick wall and her anger was at a three and it was only knee high to start with and we did the same thing with her dad and her poetry and it disappeared again, so I asked her to go back in to the memory and start the visualisation again, but she could not even see a wall or bricks or feel anything.

I had not told her that I had booked her a practical driving test as part of our therapy, let alone that it was on the next lesson as she thought we were to meet ten times before we even mentioned the "T" word again! so no one, including her, had any idea, only the DVSA and I knew. When I picked her up, I checked as always that she had her licence and told her we would do therapy second and have a lesson and mock first. She was in high spirits, right up to the point that I asked her to turn left into the test centre. We parked, and I told her no one knew she was here, no one knew she was having a test, I had paid so no one had to know that she had ever even been there that day. She knew, absolutely, that there was no pressure on her at all. Generally, she already felt happier in herself and understood, her dad had high standards, she was good at some things and her sister good at other things, so finally she finally realised that there should be no competition, and now she was going to have an opportunity to try a test when nobody even knew. She passed with just 2 minor marks and When I took her home I watched her walk to the door and, yes, her Dad's grin was massive, well, suffice to say everyone was crying, but for the right reasons.

 What we had done here, was to find out what her belief was and that was that she would always let her dad down. Her visualisation was the dark red brick wall which started bigger than she could see over, we reduced the emotion and therefore the brick wall with finding what she was good at and got her to walk over it and walk towards what made her happy which was her Dad's pride, she lost sight of the wall completely, the second time we did it a week later there was hardly any emotion or picture for her but as there was a little we did it again twice and she couldn't even see or feel it.

 The last thing for her was that I took her to test but changed the pattern, everything, no one knew, not even her and so I had changed the scenario by taking away any possible pressure caused by her actually knowing, and her parents were not waiting for a result and therefore, this was a totally different experience, there was no similarity to previous tests, her behaviour at home alerted no one and the fact that her parents did not even know that we had anything booked, meant no pressure on the day. What's more, she had gone and done something completely by herself, for herself, she trusted me (well, until the whole sudden test thing!) and she had broken a pattern that was in her head as a given outcome. It was therefore a completely different experience for the entire family, there was no pattern to match so we changed the environment and she changed her result. She text me later that year to tell me that she had passed all three A levels, she also mentioned that she was still using her affirmation six months after I set it because it was just her habit.

Chapter Twenty-one
Meditation
The pathway to the Oasis within.

What is meditation?

The word meditation often brings up images of monk like figures, sitting cross legged on a mountain top, mist swirling all around them or older images of "prophets" hanging by one leg from a tree.

Whilst you are, of course, free to adopt poses such as these if that's your choice, the aim of meditation is in fact basically to clear and calm the body and mind allowing peace and tranquillity to be achieved and making "room" in your mind for you, for reflection or silence.

This mental and physical break, during the course of a day, will improve concentration and lift your mood. Meditation carried out in a mindful way, is proven to reduce stress levels and can alleviate some of the effects of depression. The NHS in the UK are strongly behind practices such as these, which have been known, in some cases to reduce need for, or dependency on, medications and has proved for many to be a viable coping mechanism when times get tough. Meditation is an excellent tool for absolutely everyone. It is a way to remove yourself from the pressures of day to day life, relax and re-charge. Be it for ten minutes or over an hour, it is completely your personal experience, a gift that you can give to yourself. Believe me, you are worth it!

I personally, started meditating as part of my spiritual training once a week, but once I realised the difference that it was making, both to me, and to my day, I immediately adopted it as a daily practice. I now schedule my meditation in as part of my own routine, the long-term effects of such a practice are phenomenal. Some days I literally only have ten minutes once or twice a day, on others I can sit for an hour or more in meditation. The result is, without fail that I feel relaxed, uplifted, calm, peaceful and contented. My ability to concentrate is dramatically improved and little aches and pains disappear.

Meditation can be performed in various ways, by just simply "sitting in the silence" which is literally what it says, you clear all thoughts from your mind which then remains free from the general chatter it is used to, and then this time can be used instead for pure relaxation or for contemplating significant issues that you are having mental struggles with.

This is hard at first as the mind is like a monkey, you put one thought out of your mind and the next one jumps in, If you find that this is happening for you, it may prove advantageous to use pre-recorded guided meditations in the early stages, there are many on the internet or can be purchased on cd at a small cost or you can imagine or visualise, in your mind's eye, a scenario for example, going for a long walk, visualising the scenery and wildlife. Alternatively focus on the flame of a candle, either real or as a visualisation within your mind, as you sit in the quiet, some people find that listening to a purely instrumental musical track very helpful. You will, should you prefer, be able to find meditation classes available in most areas. The practice of meditation is not only being endorsed by the medical profession, but is growing in popularity naturally, now that people are learning more and more, to take control and look after themselves as a priority. I have provided, in the next chapter, an example of a full guided meditation together with details of other methods if you prefer to work on your own. Whatever means you use, practice regularly even if it seems difficult at first, if you keep this up, you will, very quickly notice an improved feeling of wellbeing, generally uplifted and more energetic.

How do you do it? Find a place and time that you will not be disturbed for however long you wish to allocate, adopt either an upright seated position, keeping the soles of your feet flat on the floor, or lie down flat on a bed, either way keeping your back as straight as possible and your neck in a straight line above your shoulders. I have known busy mums who can only manage such quiet times when they can find ten minutes to hide in the bathroom, and that is fine too, it still works, and the benefits are amazing.(Please don't lay in a deep bath to meditate, as drowning will ruin your experience),seriously though, seated upright or laying on a bed so that you are supported and safe, is essential. Close your eyes (you need to reduce as many external distractions as possible). Gently slow your breathing, a little, making each in breath deeper and slower until you feel comfortable and your body start to relax, inhale and exhale gently and you will find that this is enough to start to feel more relaxed, easing you into a more tranquil state of being.

It will feel initially, a little like you do when you are just about to fall asleep, or just coming too in the morning. It can and should, with practice, bring a feeling ultimately like you are going into a fairly deep daydream, when the ambient noises of the outside world, can just carry on by themselves and they just float away into the background, you can acknowledge them, and they will just form a gentle, barely audible backdrop to your experience.

You will be concentrating only on your breathing, or the voice if you have a guided meditation, the sound if it is an instrumental track you have, or by fixing your gaze instead on the flicker of a candle flame either watching a candle or imagining one. If thoughts come to your mind, as they will naturally early on, acknowledge and release them. Over time your own mind will get used what it is that you are doing, and it will get easier and easier to keep an empty mind which is when you can then sit in pure silence if that is your preference. Some people like to envisage themselves sitting within a bubble, totally separate and protected from the world around them. By achieving a mental state whereby your mind and body are completely relaxed. You give yourself the gift of peace, a break from responsibility, from thoughts and from activity. You are literally giving yourself time to relax, recharge and allowing your mind and body some essential love and respect.

If you manage and enjoy sitting in complete silence, (some people do, and others prefer, music, chanting or a guiding voice), then you are really taking yourself deep inside to connect with your soul, your authentic self, the one that is unaffected by ego, this is the real you, no outside influences. This allows you to do many things, perhaps just enjoy being right there, in touch with yourself, a very honest and peaceful time, others use this to mentally go to each area of their body, checking for signs of stress, little niggles or pain, either physical or emotional, this can be very healing in itself. Alternatively, this is a time, when the world is shut out, to consider something that needs reflection, perhaps something negative happened in your day and here, in the quiet you can replay the event and look at what learning there may have come from it. Allowing it to be filed without future impact on you. Maybe a big decision needs to be made, again, when you are alone in a safe environment you can give yourself the opportunity to fully consider such a decision thoroughly. The healing properties of this practice are vast and if you can make yourself important enough to make time for you in this way then you will not believe the benefits that you will very quickly start to feel.

Once you have finished your meditation it is advisable to take a moment or so to readjust, and sip a little water, as you will have cleared your body and mind of all the mental and physical stress, "noise" and general "clutter" and bought yourself to a very quiet place. You will have lowered your energy. You will feel no benefit if you immediately jump up run upstairs, make a difficult phone call and start hoovering like mad. Do those things first and after your meditation give yourself some time to enjoy this calm, tranquil feeling. After even just a week or so, you will notice your body and mind will relax more quickly into your meditation all on their own. When you very first start you may notice a tingling feeling in your feet, legs hands or arms. This feeling is no more than the body adjusting. Whilst we run around day in day out blood is pumping round the body and our heart rate increases, when we meditate the body slows down. The rate at which the heart beats slows because sending blood rushing round the body is not so essential. it's a little like when we sleep, so with less blood being pumped so hard round the body our extremities may tingle a little whilst your body adjusts. If you find this, then just before your meditation tap your feet on the floor for a moment or so and shake your hands and this keeps the blood flowing longer and will get rid of the feeling, I had this for about the first five times that I meditated and then my body got used to the fact this was rest time and I have never had it since.

Chapter Twenty-two.
Self-Guided meditations and themes.

Sitting in the silence.

This may not be something which you find easy to begin with and you may want to start with a little more structure, but once you can create your special place and turn your awareness inwards, allowing any ambient noise of the outside world to purely drift away into the background, then you can start to use this type of meditation if you feel comfortable with it. It can be used to completely clear your mind and you will, once proficient, be able to hold a completely empty mind, aware only of your own breathing, its rhythm, how the breath feels as it enters and leaves your body and how the rest of your body feels as you start to relax.

Stay in this space for as long as you feel comfortable and when you are ready to come back to the present time simply allow those ambient sounds of the world outside of you, to gently drift back into your awareness, give yourself a couple more minutes and then slowly start to wiggle your fingers and your toes then roll your shoulders, very gently, stretch a little if you need to, and only when you are completely ready open your eyes. At this point give yourself just a few minutes to re-acquaint yourself with the room you are in, the temperature of the air and check in mentally with your body from your feet up to the top of your head and see how it is feeling. Only after giving yourself this time sip some water and go about the rest of your day, knowing that both your body and mind will be rested, refreshed and very grateful to you for taking care of it – taking care of you.

Guided Meditations.
These can be bought on cd, or they can be listened to on the internet. You can find a meditation group or professional who offers one to one guided meditations, they are exactly like the visualisation below, but the facilitator talks whilst you concentrate on your breathing and listening.

Visualise a relaxing experience.
If you are just starting out with meditation or, if you struggle with sitting in the silence, then another option is to guide your meditation yourself. If the mind doesn't naturally want to stay quiet or, even if you just prefer this method you can just as effectively bring your body and mind to a quiet, calm place by taking it on a journey. What you are doing here is to stop the general chit chat that your mind will be hearing all day long and literally take yourself mentally on a tiny holiday or day out. You will be giving your mind something to think about, but rather than it be the argument you had this morning, your unpaid tax bill, the fact that the dishwasher is not working, or whatever else is happening right now, you can choose something that you would find relaxing or calming if you were to physically do it. You are going to visualise walking in nature, walking along the waterline, on a beautiful far away beach, hiking over the hills or whatever it is that relaxes you personally.

When we talk about visualisation it is a very individual thing. Some people have the ability to paint a picture vividly in their mind so that in their minds eye they see the exact scenario being described. Other people cannot see an image, I am one of them, I describe to myself in great detail what I am "visualising" and then I feel it, so for example if I imagine walking on a sandy beach I might say to myself 'I am walking slowly, along a beautiful, deserted beach, I feel the fine, white sand under my feet moving gently with each step, the sand feels warm, but as I stray a little into the gentle lapping wave, that barely reaches my toes, the water feels cool'. My body will hear the words and I start to become aware of the physical sensation in my feet, so although I am giving myself something to think about it is a beautiful, gentle relaxing single thought. All my stress dissolves and afterwards my physical body still feels as relaxed and as if it has been treated to a day out because of the detail that I have imagined.

I know that I have said this before, but it is worth reiterating here, Although our conscious mind is aware of what we are doing right now, our subconscious mind can't tell the difference between thought and reality, therefore if you tell this part of your mind that it has had a long gentle walk along the beach, it will believe you and it will respond by calming the body and the mind because of the rest that you have just given it. (see the visualisation technique section for more information on this).

An example
The following is an example of a full meditation that you can use. Once you are comfortable with this process you can envisage any relaxing, quiet, gentle experience – remember you want your mind to quiet and relax not get all excited and manic. So, keep the words that you are thinking slow, clear and deliberate,

you are using your mind to calm your body and thought
process now.

A walk in nature.
 Close your eyes and gently start to slow your breathing.
Each breath comes slower and gentler than the last. In
and out.in…and out… now bring your awareness to
that breath, notice this slow gentle rhythm which now
manages itself. Notice now how much your lungs need
to expand to facilitate this breath which enters and then
leaves your body. Notice how much your chest rises
and falls with each breath and the lack of effort to expel
the air from your lungs.

 Become aware now of the chair you are sitting in (or
bed you are lying on) feel how it supports you, holding
you still and safe in order that you can just relax, you no
longer have to be aware of it, it is there. Now, feeling so
much calmer imagine yourself sitting on a huge
oversized arm chair, there are big soft cushions all
around you making you feel so very comfortable. You
notice that the room you are sitting in is empty except
for this chair and its comfortable cushions. On the
ceiling above your head is a single light, which
illuminates you, this light wraps you in a completely
pure, white light as if offering you a blanket of
protection as it encircles you.

 As you look at the walls they are all painted white and
hold no pictures or decoration of any kind. Three flat
walls and one, the one directly opposite you has a
doorway in the middle of it, the door is made of solid
oak and has black door furniture, a large handle on the
right-hand side as you look at the door. See yourself

now getting up from this comfortable chair and its abundance of cushions and walking slowly towards the door. As you get closer, so the door appears to get larger and it looks as if it will be very heavy. You take the handle in your right hand and push the door open, it surprises you with the ease with which it moves away from you gently and silently.

You step over the threshold and immediately notice that the sun is high in the sky, it is a warm spring day and this powerful sun warms your face and makes you smile. As you take the first couple of steps you notice that you are walking on a gravel path, tiny, smooth stones move under your feet with every step and you hear the gentle crunch as you make your way along the path. You notice next, the most beautiful smell of flowers, as you look to both your left and your right you see that there are huge raised flower beds to both sides of this path.

As you cast your eyes over this abundant and fertile garden you notice that these flower beds are packed full of every size, shape and colour blooms, some varieties you have never even seen before, from the tiniest snowdrop to the tallest sunflower you have ever seen, you wonder at its extraordinary ability to stand so tall, so strong and yet seek out the sun and turn its majestic head to take in the warmth and nurture that is provided to the earth.

As you walk further, you notice that there is a large wooden archway ahead of you which is adorned with the every type, colour and variety of rose that you have ever seen and as you get closer to the gate you see that

it is slightly open and as you pass through it you notice
that you are now walking on grass, in an open meadow,
you hear the distant strains of bird song and you can
just hear the sound of water in the distance , as you
walk further the sound of the water gets louder and you
see ahead of you, a few trees, beyond which, you catch
a glimpse of the sun glistening on standing water and
realise that you are walking towards a vast lake,

The water that you heard was from a natural waterfall,
which enters the lake directly ahead of you. There is a
large fallen tree trunk to your right and you make your
way to it. This trunk has been fallen many years and has
settled in this resting place and you are able to sit on
this tree trunk and just take in the beauty of what is in
front of you. This Peaceful setting, deserted except for
you and the wildlife around you, squirrels busy looking
for their safe place in which they stored last season's
food offerings. Some tiny fish in the lake draw your
gaze for a moment and then you are distracted by the
sun which has moved slightly and is now bouncing off
the water at the foot of this lovely waterfall.

This place, a perfect place to leave behind your day will
wait for you to return but for now, you slide off the tree
trunk and start to make your way back past the trees
with the lake now behind you, the sound of bird song
interrupted only by the sound of crickets in the nearby
grass as you again catch sight of the stunning rose arch.
You take the last few steps towards the wooden gate,
swing it gently in the other direction this time allowing
you to walk through and again hear the familiar crunch
as your feet, once again, find the gravel path beneath
them. Slowly you pass between these two magnificent

flower beds until the oak door is within touching distance.

You turn for one more look at this stunning garden before stepping back across the threshold, into the room and close the door behind you. Feeling calm, tranquil and rested you nestle yourself down into the array of cushions that are piled up on this chair of yours and feel yourself once again supported. You close your eyes to block out that brilliant white light which once again swathes you and as you reflect on this wonderful experience of yours you start to allow the ambient sounds of everyday life to slowly interrupt your peace. Wriggling your fingers and toes, as you gently bring yourself back to the present and in your own time, open your eyes.

This is one example, you need to choose a theme which works for you. A Mediterranean beach, climbing a mountain, a hot air balloon ride, sitting in a garden with a loved one. Something which will allow you to add masses of detail and stop you thinking about normal everyday things. I have a friend who takes himself for a walk across vast American open planes, with nothing but grass and wild animals around him, whatever works for you. It is a mini-break for your body and mind.

You can see how important all this detail is, it serves a dual purpose whereby it not only provides you with a lovely, relaxing experience, but it completely blocks your mind from thinking about anything else. This personal oasis that you have just found, is the one to which this book refers. A place, away from the world, buried deep within you, the place that your own soul occupies, A place that you can visit, where you can find you, and where you go to build the strength to take back control. finding this place where you can put everything on hold as you take a journey inside your mind to the destination of your own choice.

As you practice your meditation, you will be able to use this technique, whenever you want or need to in order to remove yourself from the apparent reality of stress, depression, upset or fatigue, and upon your return you can choose the attitude with which to face the rest of your day. You have just taken yourself out of it to regain that control, not only of your thoughts and feelings, but long term, you can create the time and space in your life to deal with difficult issues, take time to prioritise, manage and change the life that you have.

I started meditating, and took baby steps day by day, within six months I had made the decisions about what my purpose was, and how I was going to follow the path which I absolutely knew I was destined for. This was all because I made me important enough to get to know, properly know, then to make changes, little by little until I had healed myself. Once I had the love and respect for myself that I deserved, I could see the world around me in a completely different light, my priorities changed and so did I.

Trust me, it is not a miracle or an impossible amount of good luck, money or status that you need. It starts with a single thought, then a change in attitude which instigates those baby steps tiny little changes every day, if you, make **you** important you will find the oasis within you, your strength will come bit by bit and when you improve your life, those around you notice and so starts the ripple in that pond, and suddenly you realise that your world can and has changed.

Chapter twenty-three
For reference

Colours, shapes and forms what do they mean?

When interpreting colours in your answers you will get a lot of information in how you really feel hidden in the way that you describe it.

Here are some basics and what they can mean, however, as mentioned before, with practice, you will soon start intuitively knowing what the colour that you see or feel means:

<u>Colours</u>

Red: Anger, rage, passion

Orange: wisdom, knowledge, an old soul

Yellow: Learning, study, studious, desire for knowledge or enlightenment

Green: Outside, nature, growth, peace, calm

Blue: healing (happening or needed) water, Outside, air

Purple: bruising, soul searching, spiritual ability, seeking inner fulfilment

White: purity, clean, a clean sheet, a new start

Black: Dark, bruising, hidden, modesty. solid

Pink: Comfort, emotion, feminine, gentle, love

Brown: Earth, outside, dirt, nature, growth

If you come up with a different colour, not listed here, or the meanings listed above do not match your feelings then, whilst in your lower energy, having slowed your breathing, ask yourself what is the first thing you can think of for that colour – your mind and body are tuned to you and you may well have pictures in your subconscious which relate to different meanings, for example, Navy blue, in your mental index may refer to school uniform or Dad's Military Uniform so be creative and ask yourself the questions.

Shapes

Circle: never ending, in a loop. Constant ongoing
Square: a unit of 4, (people or circumstances or situations), 4 walls – shut in, imprisoned, contained, a specific room
Rectangle: an extended unit of 4, similar to a square, however there may be space between family members (children at University or both parents are in your life but separated) or 4 areas of concern in different parts of your life.

Triangle: a unit of 3 (people, situations or circumstances) 2 against 1 – example mum and dad were absent, my 2 siblings bullied me etc.
Round/spherical – it Is moveable, but I don't know how or if I have the courage
Star – many points, lots of sharp edges or a complex situation

Forms.
Solid -impenetrable – I cannot see a way over or round this
Gas/mist I can see through it but afraid to take action/ this situation is closing in on me
A brick wall – An inner barrier, I cannot see what is on the other side, I don't know if I want to
A curtain – something is hidden, there is some part of the situation that you cannot see, or you do not want to look at.

Liquid – the situation is moving/ moving quickly/changing/fluid – you do not know what to expect of it

A tower – you feel imprisoned in this situation but are afraid to take the leap of faith into something different or unknown.

There are many other shapes, colours, forms etc, that you might come up with, when you question yourself. This is a very personal type of therapy, always take the first word you thought of and if you do not understand what you are getting, ask for more information and with practice and confidence you will be doing this yourself and starting to know yourself, from the inside out.

A final word from Me.

I would like to thank you for reading this book. If you have got to this point, then you know a lot about me and I hope that you have found at least some of the information contained useful. My dearest wish is that everyone who acquires a copy of this book, finds within its pages, at least one thing, that they can use to help them to create positive change for themselves. I am humbled and grateful for the opportunity of helping you make a difference. Thank you.

What's next?

Finding the Oasis within

Book 2

Finding Faith

Once I had finally stripped back the person that looked back at me in the mirror, and rebuilt myself without the layers of ego, of defence mechanisms and without limiting beliefs I needed to move on, in life, my life, and as a person.

I knew who I now was, I knew what knowledge I now took with me, but I had no idea what I was going to do with it. I had qualifications in many areas, however, I felt that there was a major part of me still to be found.

The reason that I had become broken was because I am completely heart led, but I had never protected that poor heart, and it had taken me through an experience, and unpleasant one at that, but there had to be a reason for it. I knew there must be something that I had to do in order to make sense of what I had been through, and that there must be a pathway which would lead me to my purpose. I just needed to find it.

I knew absolutely, that I could do anything at all that I wanted to, but I had no idea what I wanted to do. It was time to find something that I had faith in, but what did faith really mean to me? And where would I find it?